Traditional Publishing

The Complete Guide to Traditional Publishing

(How to Monetize Your Writing Beyond Traditional Publishing)

Jonathan Williams

Published By **Tyson Maxwell**

Jonathan Williams

Traditional Publishing: The Complete Guide to Traditional Publishing (How to Monetize Your Writing Beyond Traditional Publishing)

ISBN 978-1-998038-79-4

No part of this guidebook shall be reproduced in any form without permission in writing from the publisher except in the case of brief quotations embodied in critical articles or reviews.

Legal & Disclaimer

The information contained in this book is not designed to replace or take the place of any form of medicine or professional medical advice. The information in this book has been provided for educational & entertainment purposes only.

The information contained in this book has been compiled from sources deemed reliable, and it is accurate to the best of the Author's knowledge; however, the Author cannot guarantee its accuracy and validity and cannot be held liable for any errors or omissions. Changes are periodically made to this book. You must consult your doctor or get professional medical advice before using any of the suggested remedies, techniques, or information in this book.

Table Of Contents

Chapter 1: Traditional Publishing

1 Books earlier than printing

Ten thousand years within the past, there had been quality approximately three million human beings on the complete planet; maximum of them had been hunter-gatherers, and none of them may need to study or write. Today there are seven billion folks, and, as a minimum inside the western global, we are almost all moderately literate. (But ebook-reading remains confined, as one person positioned it, to an effete elite. Most humans don't have a take a look at books.)

When the number one tribes of hunter-gatherers started out out to relax out inside the Mediterranean Fertile Crescent, civilisation (as we like to call it) have come to be capable of make massive progress. And a few trouble like a ebook changed into an invention which occurred approximately thousand years in the past.

Those who settled beside the Nile observed a not unusual marsh plant which we now call papyrus. The stems of this plant can be cut up open and spread out into flat sheets which may be joined collectively at the left-hand factor. You might also need to then write numbers or letters in this cloth.

The problem with papyrus, but, modified into that if eliminated from the dry weather of Egypt and Greece it fast deteriorated; and it emerge as not until the invention of parchment that a extra long lasting writing ground come to be to be had.

Parchment become made from the dealt with skins of tender-skinned animals which include sheep. And the first-class parchment turn out to be crafted from the carefully organized skins of more youthful calves.

The earliest ebook which I actually have in my view been capable of deal with and have a look at closely dates from 1343. It is handwritten, and three extraordinary men labored on it; you could inform thru way of the shape of the letters. The language of the book is Latin, and it's miles entitled Regimen Animarum, because of this The Guarding of Souls. This ebook is a clergyman's manual – it tells him the way to conduct the mass, a manner to take confession, and so on. There are satisfactory three copies seemed to exist, they all barely splendid.

The Regimen Animarum is written in black ink on calf-skin vellum, and it's although in pretty particular shape, with crisp black print and all its pages complete. It probably took the three scribes a twelve months to complete the textual content, and probably 40 animals were slaughtered to offer the critical vellum.

In quick, the making of books, earlier than the discovery of printing, grow to be an high priced and difficult business employer.

2 The invention of printing

By the center of the 15th century, ebook production had reached a pinnacle, because of the truth there had been great such lots of animals available for parchment. (And not a number of professional calligraphers, both.) But paper saved the day.

Paper turn out to be an invention of Eastern cultures, in which it had been used for loads of years, but from the twelfth century onwards it unfold into the west. At first, the uncooked material of paper modified into linen rags – it modified into first-rate within the nineteenth century that wood pulp began for use – and the manufacture of paper became complex. But the uncooked cloth (linen) turned into specially considerable, and at the same time as printing turn out to be invented the production techniques for paper unexpectedly progressed.

Printing modified into not invented with the resource of students and gents: it changed into invented with the beneficial useful resource of difficult, practical men, regularly with little education but with a sharp eye for a fast dollar. If you have to have one call for the inventor of printing in Europe, that name is Gutenberg; and when you have to have a particular date for the begin of printing, 1450 is the incredible we are able to do.

If Gutenberg have become the inventor of printing, he come to be furthermore the number one casualty of this new commercial employer, or artwork, or technological information. He died bankrupt and dissatisfied, thus demonstrating a vitally vital factor.

Gutenberg, and masses of others like him, had discovered the handiest unchangeable function of the producing and e-book of books – it's miles a hard fact of life which has remained regular for over five hundred years.

The painful fact is that this. It is one component to install writing a e-book, even though it takes a big funding of time and labour. And it's miles every other issue to print it; although that too calls for ingenuity, staying strength, and capital. But the actual hassle – the really problematic bit inside the ebook business organization – is promoting the books.

As we will see unexpectedly, almost each creator, because the times of Gutenberg, has at one time or some other extensively misjudged the capability marketplace for a given ebook, and has ended the day with a warehouse entire of undesirable objects. In England, no longer such some of years within the past, a company called Dorling Kindersley concept that they had a bit gold mine inside the form of books related to the Star Wars films. Unfortunately they have been incorrect. They posted what proved to be 10 million copies too many, and the corporation collapsed as a give up result. It changed into taken over thru Pearson and have become part of the Penguin Group.

In the early days, printing became a business business enterprise which appealed to generation lovers, and via way of 1500 that that they had visible to it that printing grow to be nicely set up, irrespective of all the many troubles related to it.

In 1490, a rich younger man through the decision of Juliarius went on a go to to Venice. As he walked via the streets he turned into astonished to discover the stalls of numerous booksellers, piled excessive with posted books. Several hours later, at the identical time as his host got here to look for him, Juliarius have emerge as regardless of the reality that surfing, and become surround with the aid of the use of way of piles of his purchases. He became in all likelihood the primary severe e-book collector.

3. The first 3 hundred years

And so, via 1500, we had been nicely embarked on the age of observed out books.

Historians will allow you to understand that there were no wonderful technical advances in printing among 1500 and

1800. But there were truly a few critical trends.

In the early days, there was on occasion this sort of component as a author. Yes, there have been authors; and there were printers; and booksellers. But the printers and booksellers were regularly one and the same, the e book shop being definitely the residing room of a house, starting up immediately to the road, with a printing workshop within the decrease returned.

The economic arrangements among authors and those printer/booksellers were apparently numerous, and varied consistent with situation.

It so takes region that I paintings as a volunteer manual in a library which has an important collection of early books (together with the Regimen Animarum cited above), and the collection can offer a few useful examples for me to consult.

We recognize, from centuries-antique bookseller catalogues, that many early books had been immensely sensible – the manner to deal with a lame cow, as an example. But such 'books' had been often more inside the nature of pamphlets, which hung on a peg in the barn for 50 years, till they in the end fell aside. The books which typically will be predisposed to have survived for loads of years are those which have been prolonged, scholarly, and expensively sure. These had longer operating lives than the pamphlets, in element because of the reality they had been properly made, however also, I suspect, due to the truth they had been seldom handled and read.

In a library containing many such books, you may see at a glance that masses of them have been large thru cutting-edge necessities. Some 17th-century volumes, containing the writings of the early church fathers, had been made with pages some eighteen inches tall, 12 inches massive, and as plenty as a thousand pages thick. In a few instances the covers had been product of timber forums! Just taking the form of books down from the shelf is a primary effort.

These theological texts, written in Latin, Hebrew, and Greek, cannot have provided in massive numbers and have been likely subsidised by means of the usage of the Church or by the use of universities.

By assessment, a few greater business texts have been small – five inches via the use of 3 probable – at the way to reduce fees and keep the charge down.

In 1667, as an instance, one enterprising printer produced a small e-book entitled The City and Country Builder. This contained plans for constructing and rebuilding after the Great Fire of London

(1666); it'd properly have benefited from a larger format, but the publisher certainly idea that a quick and reasonably-priced advent to the problem may want to promote higher.

It will be that a e-book which includes The City and Country Builder become commissioned with the useful resource of a printer after he had offer you with the idea himself; or possibly an enterprising journalist suggested the concept to the printer. We don't recognize. But in 1650, in England, a fine Dr Walton (later Bishop Walton) got here up with a glowing idea for financing a notable printing mission.

Walton wanted to print a scholarly version of the Bible. Given that there has been masses talk in the ones days about the actual word of God, Walton proposed to scour the exquisite libraries of the sector. His plan have become to discover the earliest possible variations of the severa books of the Bible, in a few factor language he and his fifteen buddies need to discover. The consequences of those searches had been then to be published in such a way as to allow comparisons of the textual content to be with out troubles made, facet by way of facet at the same web page. The ensuing art work is referred to as the Polyglot Bible.

Between 1653 and 1657 Walton and his crew posted their Bible in six volumes. Each web page, which is prepared sixteen inches with the useful resource of manner of eleven, consists of the identical brief passage of the Bible in as a exceptional deal as 9 particular languages.

Several of the middle-eastern languages, which incorporates Syriac, Arabic, and Persian, had in no way earlier than been posted in England, and the typefaces needed to be crafted from scratch. Given that the shapes of the letters in the ones languages are so relatively complicated, and are located out in such small sizes (despite the size of the net internet page), the Polyglot Bible have become an incredible success.

Walton's six-quantity Polyglot Bible is one of the tremendous triumphs of English printing. Though it's far nicely really worth noting, probable, that English paper modified into not taken into consideration adequate to the challenge; after a fake start, higher materials were introduced in from France.

Dr Walton's method of financing the operation is, but, what introduced on me to mention this paintings within the first location. Walton raised the cash through inviting wealthy men to subscribe. A subscriber who supplied £10 in advance of the paintings turn out to be assured one duplicate of the finished set of volumes; £50 gave him the proper to 6 copies.

This method of elevating capital for a printing and publishing assignment modified into later utilized by Dr Johnson, for his Dictionary of the English Language, published in 1755. And seemingly enough, this sort of technique to financing a e book venture is beginning to find out favour over again, inside the twenty-first century. It's now called crowdsourcing.

The eighteenth century saw the emergence of publishers as we now understand the time period. Some extensively recognized publishing homes had been installation at that point, Longman (1724) being a working example: Longman is now owned by means of way of the usage of Pearson percentage, a huge current conglomerate.

The eighteenth century also saw the emergence of the present day-day novel. Professors of English Literature keep themselves well hired via debating, in print, the excellent information of the information of the unconventional, but some statistics will serve to make the issue. Whatever definition you select out out to apply to the term 'novel', it's far in reality true that the latter a part of the eighteenth century noticed the ebook of a few well-known works of fiction.

Here's a short listing: Samuel Richardson's Pamela (1741), Henry Fielding's Tom Jones (1749), and Laurence Sterne's Tristram Shandy (1759); the ones are some of the maximum well-known. Neither need to we neglect, of path, John Cleland's Fanny Hill (1766), a ebook which became, and in all likelihood despite the fact that is in a few quarters, considered blatantly pornographic.

4. The nineteenth century

It is cheap to finish, I think, that with the aid of 1800 the form of publishing in our times had step by step started to emerge.

In the primary area, we have recognisable writers of fiction. Second, we've got recognisable publishers. These are individuals who discover and join up the authors (or select books from submitted works), price the printers, and make arrangements for booksellers to promote the actual books.

We do now not, as but, have literary entrepreneurs, who negotiate with publishers on behalf of writers (despite the reality that there are now and again fathers, brothers, and other advisers who write to publishers on behalf of girl writers); and we do have some symptoms that the connection amongst authors and publishers isn't always always going to be a cushty one. Jane Austen, as an example, one of the maximum well-known writers of the early nineteenth century, reportedly furnished an early e-book (Northanger Abbey) to a creator, who did no longer something with it for ten years, and then she presented it returned yet again.

Consider too what a tedious and volatile business even submitting a manuscript should were in the ones days. An creator ought to need to put in writing the complete e-book out with the useful resource of hand – no typewriters inside the ones days. She might possibly, possibly, have hired someone to copy the text for her. But then the pile of handwritten paper may want to want to be conveyed to the functionality writer. The mail services of the time cannot had been fast or reliable, and the entire technique modified into fraught with chance. It's a wonder a few detail ever had been given finished.

Another essential component which changed into nicely installation via the early nineteenth century is that there was money in publishing (at least within the ones days; there's not loads now, as we are able to see).

Sir Walter Scott, at the same time as already famous as a novelist, changed into financially concerned in a printing enterprise which went bust. Scott can also want to have declared himself bankrupt, or normal the gives of rescue from his wealthy buddies, however he made it a issue of honour to repay the debts through his writing; and, for the motive that his novels continued to expose very popular, he managed to do gather his motive.

As the 19th century proceeded, the percentage of adults who may also need to examine frequently increased. And this is why writers a few books, or maybe small pamphlets, have been to promote in very massive numbers.

In 1849, as an instance, a powerful Frederick Manning and his spouse Maria have been located on trial for murder. The case became a sensational one, and their public execution attracted a large crowd, the behaviour of which appalled and disgusted Charles Dickens, who wrote to The Times approximately it. One enterprising writer issued a short however focused pamphlet about this situation; and in spite of the truth that the e-book turned into wonderful 16 pages prolonged, it is said by using one modern-day-day authority to have provided 2.Five million copies.

Another great development in the intervening time turn out to be the advent of lending libraries, which may also hire out books for a far smaller price than the value of buying a duplicate. The maximum well-known of those libraries had been run via a Mr Mudie and a Mr W.H. Smith. The latter's name remains related to a properly set up UK bookseller and stationer to in recent times.

Fiction modified into an nearly unrivalled form of amusement inside the 19th century. There have been definitely no cinemas, radio, or television. Fiction's sole extreme competitor have grow to be the theatre, which changed into to be decided excellent in towns of a few duration. This made it viable for writers to earn very high-quality sums of coins.

It is at this element in statistics that the query of copyright becomes vitally important. Copyright is a criminal concept, supported with the resource of maximum governments nowadays, which recognises that the author of a tale, or a fictional man or woman (no longer to say a image, a diploma play, et cetera) deserves to have the outstanding rights to take benefit of that artwork, at the least for a limited time. Publishers and others are generally obliged to apprehend copyright, mission to numerous outcomes.

In the UK, copyright turned into without a doubt well understood with the aid of manner of the 1660s. In 1663, the blind poet John Milton provided the copyright of Paradise Lost to a printer for the sum of £10.

In the USA, copyright grow to be additionally understood, but frequently ignored, at the least as a long way as English authors have been concerned. In reality, US publishers in massive component neglected the copyright in English books ultimately of the nineteenth century. Macaulay's statistics of England bought 4 hundred,000 copies within the US market, however the author despatched him no longer a penny.

Charles Dickens additionally suffered from piracy of his books, however took the trouble to adventure to america to whinge in man or woman.

If you need to examine the first-rate quick summary of the motive of copyright, and a sensible time frame for it to apply, have a study Macaulay's 1841 speech to the House of Commons. You can discover my private comments on Macaulay's perspectives in an essay entitled 'Macaulay on copyright' at the weblog Grumpy Old Bookman, 6 February 2006.

5. The 20th century

Allow me to remind you at this element that the only purpose for this brief historical survey of traditional publishing is to permit us to peer how writers were enabled, over a duration of a few 560 years, to find out a way to marketplace their novels (and special books) to the general public.

In the begin, in advance than books of any kind existed, a story must excellent be informed orally. The storyteller could stand within the mild of the fireplace, no question after as unique a meal as can be furnished, and tell his tale aloud. Very frequently he could use rhyming verse to make the assignment of remembering it simpler.

Then got here the development of parchment, and vellum, substances that may make a ebook healthy to final for one thousand years; however the way of writing a e-book out via hand, one duplicate at a time, modified into gradual, labour-sizable, and high priced.

Chapter 2: The First A Part Of The Twentieth Century

For consolation, permit us to divide the twentieth century into factors: first the years preceding to World War II, and then the rest of the century.

Prior to 1939, publishing trundled alongside fairly quietly. In the UK, some component called the Net Book Agreement came into pressure on 1 January 1900; it remained in stress for almost one hundred years.

This Agreement turn out to be a law which decreed that no individual may also additionally need to promote a ebook at a rate lower than that set thru the author, despite the fact that public libraries have been given a reduction. This intended that publishing became as gentlemanly a alternate as have to probably be imagined. There have turn out to be no provision for cost-cutters; competitive businessmen and deal-makers have been taken into consideration unacceptably vulgar. Small but everyday profits have turn out to be the order of the day.

Literary dealers had started to make an look inside the overdue nineteenth century, however there had been however few of them. A.P. Watt have become the primary, in 1875, but there were few groups of any take a look at before 1950. In principle, such sellers is probably guys (usually) who knew the e-book exchange properly (which maximum authors without a doubt did now not). Agents ought to therefore be nicely positioned to apprehend what constituted sincere remuneration for authors, and, for the purpose that they often knew the publishers individually and handled them on a normal foundation, they might be a long way better positioned to negotiate a settlement than could the author herself –

the author every now and then being a distressingly naïve girl within the provinces. That, at least, grow to be the idea, and as the 20th century proceeded, entrepreneurs have grow to be increasingly influential.

Publishing in the mean time changed into a in particular clean industrial commercial enterprise organization to get into, as it required as a substitute little capital; as a stop result, at any given time, there were quite a number of small organizations. In England, a author of fiction must possibly locate at least 30 feasible markets for a very precise, with not plenty to select between them. And, for the cause that it have become very hard for an interloper to discover anything something about any of those publishers, deciding on a business enterprise to method have emerge as frequently a don't forget of using a pin.

Paperbacks quite a whole lot made an appearance within the 1930s, with the founding of Allen Lane's Penguin imprint, but most books have been hardbacks. Printing changed into achieved in the antique way, with manuscripts (generally typewritten) being set in lead kind and published off in minimum runs of severa hundreds – or ideally hundreds. Indeed, for the purpose that the time spent putting in place the device determined most of the price, most printers won't grimy their system for a print run of lots a lot less than 1000 copies. And the ones, of route had to be warehoused someplace earlier than (it come to be was hoping) being shipped to booksellers.

In the primary a part of the twentieth century, as in each decade that we can study from proper right here on, there emerged a number of 'big name' authors in the fiction-publishing organisation.

These names divided into the literary and the economic. And even as it isn't always surprising how regularly the economic names were forgotten inner a few years (Baroness Orczy and Dornford Yates), it is also the case that many writers who then had a excessive literary reputation are also now ignored (Gertrude Stein, Edwin Arlington Robinson).

Publishing at some stage in this era may be properly described by using the phrase 'an profession for gentlemen'; surely, while the British writer Fredric Warburg came to write his autobiography, that modified into the perceive he gave it.

This word reflects an crucial fact approximately publishing. Outsiders, specifically more youthful human beings who've superior a love of books, frequently mistake glamour and press insurance for enterprise success and monetary significance. But the truth is that publishing has always been a piddling little commercial enterprise business enterprise, tiny in size at the same time as in comparison to each other excessive industrial organisation region, and in no way an area in which any splendid cash has been made – at least at the same time as in evaluation with simply big business corporation. The ecosystem in publishing become, and even though is, definitely suitable for the unworldly souls who assume that profits are of teen importance in assessment with the need to place up 'pinnacle books'. Not simplest that, but the most treasured ownership that a creator or a creator can private is a superb sized private income. If you phrase that your author is wearing a Bentley Drivers Club tie, it is probably not due to the reality he bought one with ultimate year's bonus. It's due to the fact he has inherited coins.

The 2d 1/2 of of the 20 th century

In the second one half of the twentieth century we start to draw closer to trendy instances, and to conditions which existed well inside the running lives of some of us.

The tendencies which emerged inside the path of this period can be summarised as follows:

Trend (i): Unpublished authors continued to be as ignorant of change-publishing practices as they had been for the duration of statistics.

Unless they took the problem to sign up for ebook-alternate journals, which embody The Bookseller (UK) and Publishers Weekly (US), there was almost nowhere for authors to collect any walking statistics of publishing exercise. (The internet changed into a long time away.) Subscriptions to those journals had been extraordinarily expensive (I need to comprehend – I modified right into a normal reader of each for more than one some years).

This lack of knowledge of the change's conventions and risks left the writers large open to exploitation through the publishers. Who were now not slow to use the opportunity. Exploitation is, of route, a harsh word, however that is what it amounted to, as serious examination of any sizable publishing agreement will show screen. A appropriate agent could prevent that worst of such exploitation. However… it continuously have to be remembered that an agent has to address a author subsequent week further to this week. An agent cannot therefore expect to be too hard to barter with after which be invited again at the same time as he next submits a e-book. The agent every now and then has to bend to the publisher's dreams, in region of the authors. (Oh, what crude cynicism, I concentrate you cry. Damn proper I'm cynical.)

Trend (ii): Paperbacks have turn out to be a critical element in the incomes of publishers and man or woman writers.

As mentioned above, the Englishman Allen Lane created his Penguin line of paperbacks in 1936, however it modified into not until about 1950 that the sale of paperbacks in reality took off. And the most dramatic traits had been in the US.

At first, paperbacks have been confined to reprints of books which had already been a achievement in hardback. But, in advance than lengthy, some enterprising businessmen, particularly inside the US, commenced to marketplace paperback originals. What is more, those new books had been sold out of doors the same old change channels: they were dispensed to petrol stations, news stands, and supermarkets.

These paperback originals had been often aimed toward the lowest quit of the marketplace, intellectually and socially speakme, and that they have been to begin with despised and feared with the beneficial aid of vintage university 'terrific' publishers. LeBaron R. Baker, of Doubleday, as soon as claimed that paperbacks might 'undermine the whole shape of publishing.'

This commentary modified into now not anything lots less than the fact, of path, but the manner wherein it changed into stated illustrates as an alternative well the thoughts-set of publishers at the time. Such guys (and they normally were men) have been now not seeking out sparkling markets, new readers, and new strategies to make a earnings. Far from it. They have been glad with the antique way of doing topics, didn't want it modified, and resented the vulgar upstarts who have been taking books into locations wherein they didn't belong. This thoughts-set persists to the present day, and it's miles as appropriate a recipe for business disaster as may be devised.

At first, the fashionable paperback publishers and the traditional ebook publishers had been separate companies. And because the brand new guys were very keen to advantage the paperback rights to installation large dealers, there has been a short period at the same time as traditional ebook publishers and their greater successful authors were the beneficiaries of bidding wars.

In 1968, for instance, Fawcett paid $410,000 for the paperback rights to Mario Puzo's The Godfather. A decade later, in 1979, Bantam paid $3, hundred,000 for Judith Krantz's Princess Daisy.

This ultimate price seems to have been a few issue of a turning aspect. It in the end dawned on the antique-time publishers that, irrespective of the fact that they had been doing pretty nicely out of those crude and vulgar new boys, they will do even better inside the event that they owned the paperback business employer outright.

From then on the wondering changed into that it changed into better for a publishing house to be 'vertically organised', i.E. To have its very personal in-house paperback branch, in desire to be 'horizontally organised', which allowed genuinely separate firms to shop for the paperback rights and take the general earnings on paperback profits.

Today it's miles exceptional the smaller fiction-publishing houses which might even remember selling paperback rights to 3 other enterprise.

Trend (iii): Literary sellers elevated in wide variety and effect.

By the time I started out my very own writing career, spherical about 1960, the existence of literary sellers became substantially recognized, but it come to be surely although viable to position up a manuscript to a creator yourself. Most of my books had been provided via entrepreneurs, but at the least times I did the challenge without help.

Perhaps this is as splendid an area as any to speak about how publishers find out the books which they in the end promote to the public (through the booksellers, of path).

I actually have formerly written at period about the ebook-desire technique in publishing houses, and you may discover a whole description of it in Chapter 2 of my e-book The Truth about Writing (available as a Kindle ebook). Suffice it to mention that, in the case of books submitted to publishers by manner of their authors, the initial studying of manuscripts has constantly been performed in pretty much as inefficient a manner as may additionally want to in all likelihood be devised.

Numerous bills have been written, through way of those who have done the interest, of what usually happens to unsolicited manuscripts (the so-known as slush pile). These eye-witness debts do not make encouraging studying. Giles Gordon, as an instance, as quick as said that once he become the slush-pile reader at Gollancz, he learnt how to inform whether or not a manuscript became any well interior 15 seconds. 'It's just a rely of workout,' he said airily.

As the 20th century moved closer to its forestall, the larger publishers out of area a few factor faith they could have had within the judgement in their non-public body of workers, and determined, in effect, to delegate to others the separation of the likely publishable from the oh-my-god. Hence the boom in the amount and have an effect on of literary entrepreneurs.

The cutting-edge-day role (2014) is that just a few publishers of fiction will bear in thoughts an unpublished novel till it is submitted thru an established agent. So at the equal time as a singular or non-fiction e-book is whole, the author's mission becomes one in every of locating an agent, in area of a writer – at the least as a primary step.

But don't consider that this task is an easy one each. Barry Turner, writing in The Writer's Handbook, as quickly as stated an agent who, in 14 years of reading 25-30 manuscripts a month, located five top ones. Another agent, at Curtis Brown, in my view received 1,two hundred manuscripts in three hundred and sixty five days, and took on just of the authors as customers.

Traditionally, a literary agent end up rewarded by way of being paid 10 consistent with cent of any settlement which the agent negotiated on the writer's behalf. But these days you're more likely to need to detail with 15 per cent.

I without a doubt have frequently remarked that being an agent is the hardest pastime of all in the e-book agency, and my opinion has no longer changed. At the threat of being defined as cynical, sour and twisted (another time), permit me advocate you to deal with your agent (if you ever discover one) as someone who is first and essential a company individual. In specific, exercising tremendous caution if requested to signal a agreement with an agent. Time became while we were all gents in the publishing international, and a handshake among writer and agent modified into enough. The parting of the strategies, if each celebration felt it crucial, emerge as effected in a well mannered way. But the ones days are long long past. A literary agent isn't your friend: he or she is a person you do agency with.

Trend (iv): For the last fifty years, amalgamation cum conglomeration has been the name of the game.

Conglomeration approach that large publishers take over small publishers, and if the specific small author's call survives in any respect, it does in order a subdepartment, or advertising and advertising label, in the large creator.

This device of massive consuming small has been large wherever publishers are located, and truely so on every factors of the Atlantic.

In 1950 there have been about 30 or forty publishers of fiction in the UK. These ranged from businesses that have been small and extraordinary via everyone, to principal groups which had been broadly diagnosed inside the book change if now not to the general public. Over the subsequent fifty years lots of the ones small businesses had been swallowed up into big ones, and in the long run into even huge ones, so that via manner of using the surrender of the century there have been, each within the US and UK, quality approximately six without a doubt effective trade-publishing businesses.

Let's don't forget some examples of the manner this amalgamation manner labored. We'll begin with the small English corporation of Frederick Muller.

The British Library information 354 books posted through Frederick Muller, the first being in 1932. In the Nineteen Fifties, Muller need to were quite a a success organization, as it published the UK model of Grace Metalious's Peyton Place, a ebook which was a massive dealer within the US as a consequence of its 'racy' content material fabric cloth. By nowadays's requirements it became about as racy as a properly managed church picnic, but you get the idea.

I had a e-book posted with the useful useful resource of Muller myself, in 1980: Counter-coup, written beneath the pen-name Michael Bradford. By that factor the business enterprise come to be absolutely in a few problem. I visited the workplace at one factor, and have become truely stunned via manner of the cramped conditions in which the employees labored. The organisation's HQ end up no longer in a venerable Georgian constructing in a fashionable part of London; it changed into out in an commercial enterprise vicinity in north London, and the workforce seemed to be housed in former sheds.

Muller at that factor have become owned through the UK television organisation HTV. But HTV in no manner managed to make a fulfillment of it, and Muller ran up money owed. There became a person known as Antony White related to the business enterprise, and within the 1980s he sold the economic employer for a nominal £1. He turned into obliged, however, to take on the enterprise's debt, which as I recall grow to be £400,000.

I wrote some other Michael Bradford e-book at approximately that point, and I changed into contractually obliged to provide it to Muller first. Antony White took me out to lunch to inform me that he didn't want to publish the ebook, which didn't misery me in particular because of the fact I'd made next to no longer something out of the primary one, and up to now as I are aware of it have become in no way reviewed anywhere. But I idea it changed into ordinary to ask me to lunch to say no, while a letter may also have sufficed.

Anyway, via 1984 Frederick Muller had merged with the agency of Blond and Briggs. And thru 1985 there were but some other desperate attempt to restructure and, no doubt, refinance the economic corporation enterprise, below the decision Muller, Blond & White.

Chapter 3: Hutchinson, You Could Marvel

Hutchinson grow to be based in 1887, and made some issue of a call for itself with the resource of way of issuing reasonably-priced versions. The first Mr Hutchinson (George) end up given a knighthood for his offerings to publishing.

On George's retirement, his son Walter took over, and he also elevated the commercial agency with the resource of the usage of acquiring severa smaller and as speedy as notably recognized organizations: together with Hurst & Blackett and Herbert Jenkins. Walter became moreover knighted. But eventually Hutchinson ended up being taken over via Random House UK.

As the 20th century proceeded, Random House UK additionally took over approximately a dozen London-based totally groups which had as quickly as been large powers in the land all on their non-public: Chatto and Windus (based totally 1855), William Heinemann, Jonathan Cape, Sinclair-Stevenson, and Century have been a number of the companies wolfed up through way of Random House UK.

Speaking of Random House UK permits me to provide you a short precis of the records of that employer within the US.

The actual founders of Random House have been energetic younger Americans, Bennett Cerf and Donald Klopfer, who set up organization in New York in 1927. They decided on the decision of their organization due to the truth they were 'definitely going to vicinity up some books at the issue at random'.

By 1958 Random House had end up a main creator of modern-day-interest books, but it although had best 100 or so personnel. But it grew and grew, particularly thru using taking on and soaking up one of a type companies, which include Alfred A. Knopf, and Pantheon Books. Today it occupies a good sized constructing at 1745 Broadway in New York City – it actually is all a chunk great from the shabby sheds in north London which were as speedy as occupied through Frederick Muller.

Random House now employs more than four,500 employees. In July 2013, Random House and Penguin finished a £2.Four billion merger to create the largest author in the international. But Random House is itself owned thru Bertelsmann, which Wikipedia describes as a German multinational mass-media enterprise based definitely in Gutersloh. It is outwardly a privately owned enterprise agency, with a complicated percentage form. It appears to me not going that absolutely everyone within the top reaches of Bertelsmann is aware about something loads about books.

So now you recognize what I recommend as quickly as I say that the facts of publishing from 1950 has been one in each of ordinary amalgamations, mergers, and takeovers.

This technique of increase with the aid of lumping collectively has brought about brilliant dangers for any creator trying to break into the monetary company. When companies merge, there's now one much less market available. And this is one an awful lot much less risk in your novel to electrify a publisher's reader.

The decreased opposition approach it is much less probably that editors will feel wildly enthusiastic about your ebook, and could bid the charge up in trying to influence your agent to offer it to them.

And these days, of path, you sincerely will need an agent. Big-time editors in massive agencies do not waste their time without-and-out novices, beginners, and (as they see it) time-wasters.

Trend (v): The rest of censorship in apprehend of sexual content cloth material.

Relaxation isn't quite the phrase. In truth, what came about within the 2d half of of the twentieth century is that censorship of sexual content in fiction modified into efficiently deserted. And if you are, say, many years antique in recent times, it's very hard as a way to respect really how large a trade that is.

In England, the Victorians in tremendous are typically taken into consideration to had been popular prudes. There are apocryphal testimonies about Victorian hostesses masking up the legs of tables with some thing like trousers, due to the fact to move away them uncovered can be indecent. These memories, no matter the fact that exaggerated, precise a certain reality about Victorian fiction.

As said above, the nineteenth-century subscription libraries have been critical belongings of profits for writers and publishers alike; and the two largest such libraries were operated via way of guys known as Mudie and Smith – W.H. Smith. It so takes area that every those guys were tough-center non-conformist Christians, with very strict perspectives about intercourse in giant. Sex, they taken into consideration, end up exceptional never stated the least bit. In fact, if you could find out a way to reproduce even as now not having intercourse, it might be practical to apply it.

These surprisingly influential guys made it easy that they have got been in no way going to tolerate any kind of sexual hanky-panky within the books which had been available of their libraries. And that state of affairs, all on its non-public, became enough to assure that every one organization writers of the time fell into line and closed the mattress room door in the reader's face.

Not best that, however there had been severa prison recommendations in pressure in England which have been designed to save you obscenity taking vicinity in literature or everywhere else. The specific statistics of what constituted 'obscenity' were by no means observed out, for this reason leaving it open to nearby magistrates to make their very non-public minds up. And if stated magistrates have been of the Mudie and Smith university, this may result in some very unusual choices.

Some time in my teenage years, within the Nineteen Fifties, a collection of magistrates in Swindon, England, ruled that a bookseller become responsible of publishing an obscene article because of the fact he had in stock a replica of Boccaccio's Decameron. This, if you have in no manner come across it, is a fourteenth-century paintings which incorporates a few one hundred brief stories numerous from the erotic to the tragic. Many of the memories satirise the idleness, corruption and sexual indulgence of the monks and nuns of the day. It is seemed by means of way of the use of students as an critical piece of literary history. But the Swindon magistrates have been having none of that. It turn out to be a grimy e-book. End of.

Most newspapers seemed the Swindon choice as ludicrous; however, fatuous or now not, it become the magistrates' interpretation of the regulation; as such, difficult to mission.

A fraction extra comprehensible had been comparable selections to punish the booksellers of numerous lurid paperbacks. Lurid, this is, within the experience that the covers featured girls in underclothes or much less, but the prose became however the same vintage constrained stuff, with none of the so-referred to as four-letter phrases in use. Hank Janson changed right into a pseudonym created in the 1940s, and changed into eventually utilized by a sequence of writers of these racy thrillers; as a minimum one such writer changed into prosecuted for obscenity.

In England, in the 1950s, most fairly mature writers, readers, and printers, have been bored stiff with the uncertainty which surrounded intercourse in books. They had no clean idea of methods far they could glide in sexual subjects. One difficulty modified into pretty easy, but: if writers used phrases together with fuck, cunt, prick, arse (ass) and all the equal vintage vulgar synonyms for sexual organs, they have been going to be in hassle. 'Serious writers' specifically determined this situation intolerable.

It were intolerable even inside the Twenties, at the equal time as D.H. Lawrence intentionally wrote a unique, Lady Chatterley's Lover, which broke diverse taboos. Lady C described in detail the sexual relationship among an uneducated jogging man and a excessive-born female, and it made good sized use of all of the forbidden phrases. A small personal model of this e-book have become published in Paris, but nobody, whether or not or now not or now not creator, creator or printer, imagined that it may then be posted in England because it stood.

In 1959 a cutting-edge Obscene Publications Act come to be surpassed thru the British Parliament. This made it possible for a ebook to interrupt out prosecution for obscenity if it modified into held to have 'literary gain'. This come to be but every unique vague word capable of greater or less any interpretation, and the following one year the English writer Allen Lane decided that it modified into time to quit the doubt and uncertainty. He therefore published an unexpurgated version of Lady Chatterley's Lover as a Penguin paperback.

The e-book of Lady C (because it come to be widely diagnosed) constituted an open mission to the regulation. And the authorities responded thru prosecuting the publishers for obscenity.

After a prolonged trial, in the front of a jury, Lady C and its publishers were acquitted – plenty to the disgust of the pick and the prosecuting suggest. From then on, folks who wrote sexual descriptions in novels felt steady in what they have been doing, despite the fact that they used formerly forbidden phrases.

Much the identical trends happened inside the US, even though with out, to this point as I am aware, this sort of clean landmark ruling. True, the Supreme Court had in 1933 declared that James Joyce's Ulysses have become no longer obscene, and this opened the door for e-book of 'extreme works of literature' which blanketed sexual description and 4-letter terms. But for some time puritanism remained the dominant pressure in US fiction.

By manner of instance, some readers can also furthermore consider Grace Metalious's 1956 novel Peyton Place (already referred to as being published through Muller in England). Peyton Place, Wikipedia tells us, end up 'reviled via the usage of way of clergy' on its first e book. In 1958, once I visited the usa, I became instructed via manner of one decent matron that she had attempted studying the ebook, and after skimming via some chapters she had inserted it into the furnace which drove the own family's vital-heating device.

Despite such reactions, Peyton Place remained at the New York Times bestseller list for over a one year. Some thirty years later, but, this wicked ebook changed into taken into consideration so tame that it changed into take a look at aloud, in every day excerpts, at the BBC's radio programme for center-elderly, middle-elegance housewives: Woman's Hour.

Nevertheless, puritanism died hard, and nowhere have become this extra real than within the town of Boston, in which the city officials had massive powers to ban a few detail that they taken into consideration 'objectionable'. Among the 20 th-century works which fell foul of the Boston city fathers' rulings had been (inevitably) Lady Chatterley's Lover, Hemingway's A Farewell to Arms, Forever Amber by using using Kathleen Winsor, and Naked Lunch, thru William S. Burroughs. (Boston additionally banned the Everly Brothers' music 'Wake up Little Susie'. Go parent.)

From the 1960s onwards, attitudes changed. And no longer best in terms of books, but additionally in phrases of what became feasible on degree and in movies.

In London, diploma plays were difficulty to strict censorship, which end up regularly completed with the useful resource of using ex-military officers of a puritanical turn of thoughts. Nearly anyone regarded this archaic tool as farcical, and in 1968 it have become in the end deserted. The musical Hair, which had earlier been refused a licence, became in the end produced on an English degree.

In the cinema, the US Hays code made it hard to portray something which would possibly quite be referred to as ordinary sexual family members among males and females, not to say something wonderful.

But times additionally changed in Hollywood, and once they did they modified suddenly. By 1979, when I visited New York for the 1/three time, I actually have emerge as capable of pay a couple of bucks and watch people having uninhibited sexual sex on a big display screen and in complete colour, right on Broadway; I became in no fear of the place being raided.

This revel in changed into, I have to confess, some aspect of a novelty. Remember that simplest a long time earlier it had been not feasible in England, and likely within the US, to find out even a nude image of a woman, in a magazine, which did not have the version's pubic hair airbrushed out of lifestyles. But in 1979 I must now see the lady's vagina, projected to a huge length on a large display display. Not remarkable that, however the lady become maintaining her vagina massive open for an erect penis to enter her. The experience of watching this modified into, as I say, some thing of a novelty; however after approximately twenty minutes I did begin to marvel whether or not there might not be higher techniques to spend my time.

The detail of this instead prolonged subsection of bankruptcy 2.Five.2 is to make it clean to you that, in which sex is involved, writers now have freedoms which have been almost impossible barely fifty years inside the past. And it has all passed off sooner or later of my individual lifetime.

Yes, of path, the query of sexual descriptions in fiction is still controversial. In October 2013, there was a massive row about 'offensive' books being made to be had through... positive, you've guessed it, W.H. Smith's on line e-book keep! What an underestimation. And you can anticipate similar rows to rumble on for ever more. There will continually be folks that regard sexual descriptions in books due to the fact the paintings of the satan, and if you write express fiction you want to be prepared to should solution for your movements sometimes.

Chapter 4: The Reason?

Please allow me to remind you, earlier than we pass any in addition, that the whole purpose of this ebook is to provide what its identify says: A Writer's Guide to Trade Publishing.

It isn't an investor's manual to publishing, or a history of publishing (except insofar as you need to have a bit of attitude at the business enterprise); and it isn't always a guide to copyright or the criminal headaches of publishing contracts (despite the fact that, through the use of some thing gods you keep steeply-priced, you could simply want the form of guide in case you are ever supplied a publishing deal).

No. This e-book is definitely one guy's view of the way matters are, and the manner we came. If I become sounding thoroughly jaundiced approximately change publishing, that's due to the fact I've been coping with publishing companies for 50 years, and feature examine greater considerably about the organisation than is right for me. I want to have been writing instead.

As a quit quit result of that manner, I even have certainly ended up jaundiced, cynical, depressed, from time to time disgusted, and virtually disillusioned. Sorry about that, but that's the way it's long gone for me. You may have higher fortune if you ever dabble in exchange publishing. Good actual fortune with that.

So, that having been said, permit's take a brief image of publishing on the forestall of the 20 th century.

The British publishing scene in attitude

Here is a summary of the United Kingdom publishing scene which I wrote for my e-book The Truth approximately Writing, posted quickly after the turn of the century. The characteristic in America, or a few different western united states of america, will be quite an lousy lot the identical at that point; the American marketplace is five or six times larger than the UK, but the proportions in every u.S.A. Would be about the identical.

One of the issues that we face in getting an define of British publishing (or some other america's identical) is that there are lies, damned lies, and information approximately the e-book company. However, here is a massive-brush image, drawn from reasonably dependable resources.

If we overlook about academic/professional books and faculty textbooks, and in fact think about change publishing, the customer in 2000 became placing approximately £2 billion a 12 months into the excessive-avenue tills.

That profits from the purchaser is, of route, divided. A largish chew is going to the bookseller; he receives probable 35% of the retail price for a hardback, and greater for a paperback. Another chew, in all likelihood 15%, may work to the wholesaler who supplied the bookseller. As a result, a publishing agency is probably doing properly if it managed to position its hands on 50% of the cash spent with the useful resource of the excessive-road e-book-client. In many companies they may be pleased to get 45%.

We also can consequently count on that UK exchange publishers had been re incomes about £1 billion a year.

At first sight this seems to be a huge sum. But, in case you have a look at this discern with the profits of groups in exclusive industries, you'll without delay see that, in enterprise and enterprise terms, publishing is a small enterprise.

For example: the income of all of the businesses of solicitors (prison specialists) inside the UK is £11 billion a 12 months; the Shell oil enterprise has an income of about £a hundred billion, i.E. A hundred times as large as all UK alternate publishers prepare; and, in its 2000 posted file, Barclays Bank recorded a profits of virtually £four billion. And Barclays wasn't even the maximum important UK monetary institution – it modified into the fourth largest.

In addition to being a appreciably small earner, publishing is likewise a small agency. Faber, one of the most well-known names in the e-book international, at that aspect hired simplest one hundred twenty 5 people. Even Hodder Headline, one of the top 1/2-dozen corporations, employed an lousy lot a whole lot much less than 800.

Compare those figures with almost some other business enterprise and you can see that the numbers are tiny. In Wiltshire, in which I turned into residing in 2000, there can be a small metropolis referred to as Trowbridge. The largest business enterprise in Trowbridge is a manufacturer of beds, known as Airsprung. This company employs 1,000 humans, and you will surely in no way have heard of it; in reality you probably haven't even heard of Trowbridge.

In financial terms, trade publishing is not a worthwhile commercial enterprise to artwork in. A Bookseller survey in 2001 hooked up that the commonplace earnings paid to those elderly among 19 and 23, who were of their publishing jobs for much less than a 3 hundred and sixty five days, modified into £14,416. (Nearly these sort of groups are based totally absolutely in London, don't forget.)

In one medium-sized alternate writer, the overall not unusual sales became genuinely below £20,000, with the nice-paid director taking domestic some £45,000. By manner of contrast, a educate cause force on the London underground have grow to be then earning approximately £31,000 a yr. There are a few publishing bosses who earn over £a hundred,000 a twelve months, however not many.

Because of its low incomes power, and pathetic profits margins, publishing is of little interest to the City of London. Generally speakme, the business enterprise gives a terrible flow back on capital. A record published in 1999 stated that handiest 32% of publishers made an 'ideal' move lower back of 10% on their funding, and that about one zero.33 of publishers have been 'grossly inefficient' in their use of capital.

In brief, whilst we endure in mind the economic data, coupled with employment statistics, we find out that publishing is a piddling little company of very little impact to each person. When in assessment with the oil agency, banking, or insurance, it is minuscule.

Publishing is, but, a commercial company this is performs an in truth important thing in what might be called the kingdom's manner of life, and it has a large characteristic in schooling. It furthermore attracts a disproportionate quantity of newspaper location; this misleads almost certainly anybody into wondering that a well publicised e book makes its writer wealthy. Ah, if simplest!

A quick evaluation of the manner the contemporary large businesses had been doing inside the one year 2000. These new massive boys had been going to make a good deal larger income, you maintain in thoughts, than the multitude of smaller organizations whom they had wolfed up. At least, that changed into the concept. (Excuse me while I clearly have a quiet snigger.)

We noted above that, via the late 1990s, the way of amalgamation amongst publishing corporations turn out to be properly advanced, every within the UK and inside the US.

In London, there had been seven or eight corporations that may each declare approximately 3 in keeping with cent or more of the general retail marketplace. The largest of these were Random House, Penguin, and HarperCollins. Companies which had as quickly as been owned via manner in their eponymous founders (Gollancz, Deutsch, Weidenfeld), were now managed with the beneficial aid of a curious aggregate of 'hard-headed' businessmen. Of the maximum important organizations, have been traded without delay or in a roundabout manner on the London stock exchange, were German-owned, one US-owned, one Australian, and one modified into the subsidiary of a French fingers manufacturer.

In the US, the state of affairs become possibly even extra manifestly centralised. While there have been many small publishers ultimate – some of them started out up because of the reduced charges related to new printing strategies (see beneath) – six big companies ruled the scene. For a decade or so the ones agencies had been stated, with awesome originality, due to the fact the Big Six.

The scenario changes unexpectedly, and in 2013 the Big Six have turn out to be the Big Five, via the merger of Penguin and Random House. So in case you want to avoid confusion I am going to explain the us Big Five/Six as they may be at the time of writing (early 2014).

The firms worried are Random House plus Penguin (now mixed), Simon and Schuster, HarperCollins, Macmillan, and Hachette. Only of the Big Six are US organizations: Simon and Schuster, and HarperCollins. The others are foreign places: are German, one is British and the alternative is French.

Some of those agencies are quoted on the stock exchange, but it is an instance of the terrible profits data of large-time publishers that maximum stock-market observers experience that the share expenses of the determine groups of those companies would likely rise well if the dad and mom dumped their children.

Simon & Schuster, a call to inspire ecstasy inside the ebook worldwide, is simply a drag on the percentage charge of CBS. And

Wall Street would love News Corp a whole lot higher if it really offered HarperCollins.

Random House, as quickly as a proudly American agency, is now owned by the use of Bertelsmann, a agency which modified into as quickly as the maximum critical writer of Nazi propaganda; and, moreover, the employer's earnings benefited from the slave labour furnished to them through the Nazi celebration. But that turned into all a long term age, and out of the country, so we received't make a fuss about it now, can we? Wouldn't quite be sincere, would it?

From the point of view of ought to-be writers, none of this is proper records. Once, well internal my individual lifetime, a writer also can want to pretty supply off her manuscript to as many as 30 publishers; and best if she became rejected with the aid of the use of the use of they all may want to she need to impeach her religion that her terrific ebook could likely definitely discover a domestic soon. Today, you want an agent to get any of the powerful businesses to study your stuff in any respect. And probable it'd excellent take three or four rejection letters to settle the matter in your agent's thoughts.

Within the Big Five, properly informed and properly look at males and females no longer make alternatives approximately the fee of novels and biographies. Calculations are as an opportunity made via way of TV-watching bean counters, proudly owning approximately as a extraordinary deal tradition as a warm canine and a can of beer.

In 1990, Random House became now run not with the resource of a literary chap, however through manner of the usage of a former banker named Alberto Vitale. He changed into a person who boasted to anyone that he become a long way too busy ever to have a look at a ebook. In that 365 days, Vitale determined that he preferred to get rid of Andre Schiffrin, an prolonged-standing and plenty famous head of a Random House literary department. To gain this, Vitale surely 'rearranged' a few Random House costs, charging Schiffrin's division for charges which had actually been incurred a few special place. Schiffrin's backlist of books, probably a first rate asset, changed into written off at zero value. Result: Schiffrin changed into recognized as a hopeless loser of the employer's coins. He changed into kicked out.

If this is how the large corporations of these days deal with their distinguished workforce, how involved do you trust you studied they are inside the profession of an unpublished author which includes yourself?

Even their published writers get what ought to probable courteously be referred to as the dirty prevent of the stick. Consider the future of technological know-how-fiction author Mary Doria Russell. Mary started out to be posted through the usage of Random House in 1996. She did 5 novels with them, prevailing an Arthur C. Clarke award and an ALA Readers Choice award. Entertainment Weekly selected her ebook The Sparrow as one of the ten outstanding books of the yr.

Just as her new novel Doc modified into released in 2011, Mary obtained word that Random House became no longer interested in any greater books from her.

There were no previous indication that this choice emerge as coming close to near.

Fortunately, Doc modified into well reviewed and changed into decided on as one of the Washington Post's top 5 novels of 2011. Now she is posted with the resource of the use of an imprint of HarperCollins. So all's nicely – after a fashion. But after the Random House experience it took her, she says, approximately 3 months to respire proper. 'I'd been so happy there. The income people have been first rate with me. But there has been some of churning with editors. I'd had nine editors for my 5 novels.' And what hundreds of fun that need to have been.

Moral of all this: In in recent times's global of the Big Five (or the Big One and 4 others, as a few human beings do not forget it – it's no specific being a outstanding practitioner in a small-promoting area of hobby style. Today you have to deliver blockbusters, on which the whole thing is based upon, otherwise you're out for your ear.

Mary Doria Russell has a web internet website online online with an 'recommendation for aspiring authors' segment. It is critical analyzing for honestly each person studying this e-book.

And then there are those sneaky clauses inside the large corporation's settlement that you haven't really observed. In the very week that I wrote this section, a historically posted writer wrote a blog publish beneath the name 'Honesty positioned up: a mean traditionally published author's pay.'

In this put up, the author set out the entire info of what she had earned over the preceding 3 years with HarperCollins.

Within four hours, this post became taken down. Publishers, you spot, don't locate it impossible to withstand while an creator famous how pitifully small their profits often are. It upsets the suckers who may additionally additionally in any other case provide them books.

The author later placed that she had to take the publish down for 'agreement disclosure motives'.

Some publishers (probable all, come to do not forget it), insert a non-disclosure settlement into their agreement. They don't want authors speakme approximately the coins.

By 2000, the antique publishing device come to be pretty a whole lot broke(n) except, and writers had been now not glad approximately it.

Luke Johnson, a former Chairman of Channel four television in the UK, had previously been a publisher. He described his time in that task as 'a painful revel in.' Generally, he said, publishing is a 'horrible commercial organisation… a barely rational corporation.' And he grow to be dead right, of path.

Across the Atlantic, skilled writers have been feeling highly sad with the consequences of publishing's travails over the preceding a long time. Warren Murphy, a famous American creator who had written dozens of books and had acquired Edgars (crime fiction's Oscars), described how he had but to be paid for his modern-day e-book (which have emerge as then in the shops). 'In the old international of publishing,' said Murphy, 'writers always come remaining.' And he wasn't talking about intercourse. He changed into talking approximately getting paid.

Murphy went without delay to forecast the loss of life of publishing, as presently constituted. 'Editors who can't edit... Bookkeeping practices that might befuddle Stephen Hawking... An organisation whose industrial business enterprise practices have been vintage a hundred years in the past and dumb even in advance than that.'

And it wasn't absolutely the commercially minded writers who've been bored stiff. In 2001 V.S. Naipaul become presented the Nobel Prize for Literature. But a few years in advance he has given an interview wherein he said, 'My grief is that the publishing worldwide, the e-book writing global, is an surprisingly shoddy, grimy, dingy international. There are in all likelihood simplest three or 4 publishers in London that one has any regard for. The others have the morality and the manner of lifestyles of barrow boys – street sellers, human beings pushing rotten apples.'

But, spherical approximately the stop of the 20th century, exchange emerge as in the air. Whether publishers knew it or no longer it, trade was rolling inexorably alongside.

Two elements of the approaching alternate

In late 1999, publishing stood on the edge of revolutions. Both of them had been essentially technological.

On the only hand, it changed into with out difficulty obvious, at least to genuinely genuinely every body who turned into paying any intense interest, that a primary change in printing era, in choice to, say, e-book distribution and retailing, emerge as already beneath way.

Printing had remained extra or less the identical way given that Gutenberg in 1450. In 1810, the usage of steam to energy the presses were delivered; ;this enabled them to paintings masses quicker and ultimately reduce expenses. But considering the fact that then, not something new. Type became but set in lead, and after the primary model of the ebook became posted you still had to determine whether or no longer to store the trays of lead (highly-priced), or to allow the steel to be melted down.

But now… In the overdue Nineties, a technique known as Print on Demand (POD) become already widely available, and about to emerge as more so.

POD have become a laptop-based totally approach. Text have become entered at once to a computer's hard electricity, along side a thousand or special books, and on the identical time as you desired a reproduction – positive, even a single replica – you in reality pressed a key and a glorified Xerox device revealed one off for you.

Time: about fifteen minutes.

Result: large discount in printing costs. Less investment required, a whole lot an awful lot less risk. For a e-book which needed a primary printing of one million copies in paperback, the vintage way of printing modified into nevertheless a good deal less luxurious; however the technique of massive change become no matter the truth that truly obvious.

Apparent, this is, and as I stated in advance, to each person who changed into paying hobby. Most human beings in publishing weren't doing that. And regardless of the reality that they sensed the coming of exchange they were decided to prevent it.

Around the flip of the century, Jason Epstein wrote a e-book entitled Book Business; it have become published 2001 in the US. This ebook became an exam of present practice in publishing, and a much-sighted glimpse into the destiny. Epstein was quite well certified to install penning this form of e-book, due to the fact he were editorial director of Random House, in New York, for 40 years.

It turn out to be moreover across the turn of the century that I myself, in England, turned into putting in location small organisation of my non-public, mainly to position up my very very personal books, under some of pen-names; I alleged to take whole advantage of the latest POD generation. This mission concerned me talking to wholesalers, printers, booksellers, special publishers, library employees, and, not least, readers. Wherever I went I asked as many humans as I may want to whether or no longer that that they had have a observe Epstein's Book Business. I in no way determined all and sundry who had.

This did not marvel me, due to the reality through then I had concluded that the individuals who worked within the ebook business commercial enterprise organization have been, as humans, a satisfaction to understand, humans whom you may welcome as neighbours, and perhaps at the identical time as suitors in your daughter's hand. But as specialists, income-makers, prolonged-time period business enterprise strategists – truly hopeless. Clueless past redemption.

Even at the same time as his e book have become published, Epstein had already concluded that successful writers didn't want publishers the least bit. People like Stephen King and Danielle Steel, with fairly a achievement tune data, need to pretty with out trouble have reduce free from sellers and publishers, and will have offered in such capabilities as they wanted, in terms of editors, e-book designers, printers, e-book distributors, and so on. By doing just so they might probable have earned a notable deal more at the give up of the day. In workout, but, at that stage, they all decided on to keep doing subjects the vintage manner – however which have end up in all likelihood as it best their consolation to accomplish that. (Either that or they weren't paying any hobby every.)

Epstein grow to be a large POD fan, and he anticipated a scenario wherein a smooth coffee preserve for your close by excessive street would likely have a printing gadget parked on the once more. You may come within the door, order a coffee of your choice, and then order the ultra-modern J.K. Rowling to take out with you fifteen mins later. That association has now not pretty come to fruition but, but there's now a agreement in stress among Xerox and Kodak to run this sort of facility through the Kodak photographic printing shops.

The beginning of ebooks

A 2nd recreation-changing development have come to be already being notion about via the few enterprising publishers who were now not certainly unaware of computer technology. This changed into the possibility of studying books on a pc display screen as opposed to on paper. It changed into the approaching of virtual books, or ebooks as we now think about them.

Consider, with the aid of way of example, the usa enterprise enterprise Renaissance E Books, which changed into based in 1997. This company modified into without a doubt one of the earliest publishers of ebooks at the internet. In 2003, hastily earlier than his loss of life, the real founder of the company offered the industrial employer to a consortium which appointed a widely known publishing editor named Jean Marie Stine to run the display. And run it she did, thoroughly.

Shortly after Jean Marie took price, I signed some of contracts with Renaissance to submit a number of my very very own books in virtual codecs (prolonged earlier than the Kindle, please be aware); the ones contracts have been models in their kind.

In the early days, ebooks have been often offered in pdf layout. But you didn't need to be very bright to peer that, as quick as a surely inexperienced and without problem transportable e-book reader changed into advanced, some component that you could supply spherical on your pocket or handbag, the sale of ebooks need to in reality take off. More of that later.

The purpose of phase 2.6 has been to advantage an define of trade publishing on the very forestall of the twentieth century.

Publishing companies are first and most crucial companies. That is to say, their motive is to make coins for the shareholders. As such, their commonplace performance has continuously been somewhere among awful and pitiful. For an examination of British publishers, seen from this attitude, please see Eric de Bellaigue's 2004 e-book, British Book Publishing as a Business for the cause that Sixties.

Chapter 5: Writers Really Want It Besides?

The effect of the virtual age

This e-book is being written in 2014, sort of fifteen years for the reason that flip of the century, a period which we handled in Part Two. Part Three therefore seems at the effect of generation on the publishing company at some point of the crucial years for the reason that 2000.

Like it or no longer – and a few human beings hate it – the final ten years particularly have seen big adjustments in the publishing organization, and it's far instructive to evaluate what has occurred there to what befell in distinct industries that have been converted with the aid of virtual strategies.

Consider the enterprise of pictures. You can not often fail to have observed that these days every body from the age of six upwards has a virtual virtual digital camera. And you've likely located that antique faculty film has almost vanished from the shops. Grandma no longer contains a boasting ebook entire of snapshots of her grandchildren: as an alternative she has an iPad or a tablet, and she whizzes through the piccies with the useful resource of the usage of swiping her arms across a display screen.

What you could no longer have observed, unless you're very eager on photographs, is that each one this changed inside clearly a completely few years. More to the factor, some noticeably well-known photographic agencies certainly went out of industrial agency – they have been swept away via the surge of virtual trade. Legendary companies which includes Polaroid, Bronica, Contax, Agfa, Konica, Minolta and Ilford all withered and died.

Christian Sandstrom did a few research into what brought on this industrial disaster; and he installation that it wasn't due to the fact the organizations ignored digital tendencies. Far from it. They tried to get in the sport. But they failed due to the fact their tough-won abilities and organization revel in have end up beside the issue within the new market. One Hasselblad employee knowledgeable Sandstrom that he have to never have imagined that the shift would possibly take location so rapid and with such implications. Fundamentally, the older photographic businesses failed due to the fact their middle competence turned into not associated with electronics, and due to the fact they were overtaken with the resource of the rate of sports.

Plenty of different industries were suffering to deal with virtual trade, and some studies in this phenomenon has been executed in academia, considerably via the use of Harvard organization professor Clayton Christensen.

A number one instance, in an agency that is highly greater in period and significance than e-book publishing, is the disaster which hit the manufacturers of mainframe laptop systems, whilst the producers of minicomputers got here at the scene. And those manufacturers of minicomputers had been in turn threatened with the resource of the manufacturers of personal laptop systems; and pills, and smartphones, and all like that.

The maximum crucial trouble is that digital trends make the whole thing less expensive. Consumers love this, however it creates crucial problems for those who had been doing subjects the vintage way, and would really like to move on doing matters the vintage way, thank you very an lousy lot.

The present corporations have to be virtually, surely clever to stay on. And do huge publishers strike you as being without a doubt, certainly smart? Come on now, it's a extreme query.

The researchers inform us that almost nobody from the vintage order is capable of undertake the essential adjustments to live on inside the new order. When the area modifications and the company doesn't, the organisation has a tendency to disappear.

So, in which does that leave conventional ebook publishing?

In problem, that's wherein. Anything in addition a protracted way from virtual competence than a modern-day-day publishing organisation might be quite hard to locate; and, as anybody understand, they're no longer precisely brief on their ft each. So, because of the reality the years went thru, many observers, which encompass myself, commenced out to feel that old fashion change publishing would likely short die the demise. To tell the truth, we weren't too thru that notion.

Well, catastrophe for the Big Five (and others) hasn't quite passed off. Not yet. But the dinosaurs in publishing are doing their fine to assist it alongside. It took them a long term to workout consultation the manner to ship emails, no longer so very lengthy in the beyond, and truly an internet internet page wasn't in reality essential, end up it? Just a fad. Would in no manner seize on.

Watch this region.

How to sell a e-book to a traditional writer

Here's how the commercial organisation labored at the surrender of the 20 th century, from a author's thing of view. And this is the way it nonetheless works. Sort of. 'Works' is a relative term.

Writer spends masses of hours jogging on a very specific. Possibly from 1990 to 1995, permit's say. Then, in 1996, the author attempts to approach publishers – first-rate to find that they normally don't keep in mind books sent in thru manner of nobodies. Even those corporations which do receive submissions motel to a few exciting dodges.

The Galleycat weblog suggested that a few groups invent fake editors, who ship out rejection letters on the company's behalf. One editor suggested that, 'A enterprise that I worked at within the '90s not simplest sent out rejection letters underneath a faux editor's name, but this faux editor moreover had a voicemail container and an e-mail deal with.' If a writer complains approximately her remedy, she can be suggested that Mr Smith has left the corporation.

So, no longer getting everywhere with an immediate approach, our creator gadgets out to find a literary agent who can technique without a doubt considered one of publishing's gatekeepers with out stated gatekeeper collapsing into tears of laughter. Agent, as soon as found, and once satisfied that he has some detail which may likely, with appropriate fortune, show best, sends the e book to his bestest tremendous pal. Pal accepts. Book published! Reviewers find it not possible to face up to! Bookshops stack it on the the front table. Fame and fortune observe! Hurrah. Nobel prize and any others of phrase are presented with out argument. No contest. Big interviews on TV and in major newspapers. Your neighbours beg you to come back to dinner. In your chauffeured Rolls Royce

And, once more, all like that.

That's what you consider. But of path, that isn't the way it is going.

The search for an agent can take years. Even while positioned, the agent indicates changes. These take months, if not years. Despair gadgets in, however you warfare thru.

Revised e-book is despatched out. Gets rejected. Often takes years to discover an editor who is concerned.

When found, the editor desires changes. Funnily sufficient, she desires our creator to exchange matters once more to the way they had been in the first version (despite the fact that the editor doesn't recognize that). After more tears, destroy-up with boyfriend due to the fact he in no way sees you, you do the changes. Agent sends off new edition. Editor sends a be conscious to say she is leaving the organisation and her opportunity doesn't similar to the ebook. Sorry.

After or 3 iterations of this, not often taking extra than approximately a decade, you in reality get supplied a settlement. Wow! At ultimate! Virtue, tough paintings and obsession are in the long run rewarded. Terms of settlement appear a chunk harsh, however you make a decision not to argue. You yearn to be posted.

Months skip. No one talks to you approximately a few factor – agent and editor all too busy. Then someday, you get preserve of a difficult and rapid of proofs. To be examine, corrected and again in a unmarried day please. You struggle to comply. Send decrease lower back proofs. Further months pass. A determined reproduction of the ebook arrives. You hate the cover. Wasn't there a few issue within the agreement about cover approval? Yes, says agent, but no individual takes that critically, and anyways the dust jackets are all found out now.

Publication day arrives. Nothing takes region. No release birthday party, no opinions for months, the book store close to your house has in no way heard of your e-book and doesn't need to inventory it while you describe it.

Contract calls for a few different e-book. You repeat the procedure. Same aspect happens: i.E. Not something. One day agent sends an e-mail to mention that income were disappointing and writer doesn't need you any more. Given this, says agent, and the overall united states of america of the market, the agent doesn't want you any greater every.

End of 'profession'. But it's all been such amusing, hasn't it? You wouldn't have unnoticed it for the worlds, have to you?

You think I exaggerate, don't you? Ah, if you most effective knew. That's the fantastic version.

At the immediately you watched that is genuinely me, being nasty and cynical and bitter. Well, in the end you may discover. The hard manner. Or perhaps not, in case you're clever.

three.Three How the Kindle changed everything

On 19 November 2007, Amazon launched the Kindle. The Kindle changed into the number one little laptop thingy which have become designed basically for studying ebooks, and there need to had been a collection of people obtainable looking ahead to it as it supplied out in five and a half of hours. Even at $399. The device remained out of inventory for the subsequent five months.

But how did this affect writers? Dramatically is the solution.

Prior to 2007 it had continuously been possible for a author to place up a e-book herself, in traditional posted form. It have emerge as very clean, furnished you were organized to throw loads of cash round. The difficult element became selling your e-book to readers.

Bookshops could possibly now not need it, even though you can get access to 3 dependable distribution device. So as often as no longer you gave away a hundred copies in your own family and friends and stored the opportunity 9,900 on your garage. Where they stayed for the subsequent ten years, till you ultimately typical the inevitable and paid to have them carted away for pulping.

But now, with the advent of the Kindle, Amazon made it viable for each person –

actually absolutely everyone – to put up their non-public e-book. And how a whole lot did it rate? Nothing. Oh sure, you may spend money on professional enhancing and evidence-reading if you needed, pay for it to be formatted and for a fancypants cover format, but you didn't need to pay for any of that. You ought to do all of it your self. And how a good buy did a DIY approach price you? Nothing. Not a penny.

Furthermore – and this is the almost awesome detail – Amazon virtually want you to submit your e-book via their centers. There are not any editors asking you to rewrite the surrender, and on the equal time as you're at it, reduce 20,000 terms out of the whole lot. Instead, you may publish some thing you rattling properly please, and welcome, from a one-internet web page poem to a 250,000-word literary masterpiece inside the fashion of James Joyce.

Yes, it is real that a ebook about perverts having intercourse with youngsters and dogs will probably get you unpublished by using way of Amazon. And too much scatological libel approximately lots cherished public figures will likewise enhance some eyebrows inside the Amazon workplace. But whatever that is is fairly, and a good deal that isn't, will normally be well-known.

Just thru way of way of instance, some or three years inside the beyond I got here throughout an author who modified into publishing brief novellas of about 10,000 terms. These have been selling about 2,500 copies a month – no matter the fact that the lady couldn't spell or punctuate to preserve her lifestyles. No conventional writer's reader should have have a have a look at multiple paragraph of her paintings. But on Kindle she need to place up and sell.

And who, you may moderately ask, have become searching for such semi-literate rubbish? Answer, people who've been semi-literate themselves, however desired to be cautioned a wonderful story. And they had been studying those books on their smartphones. These readers didn't care about the spelling and the punctuation, because of the fact they were in no manner plenty unique at that stuff at faculty, and that they aren't about to start being fussy approximately it now. Just tell us a tale, please Miss, and we'll be very grateful.

In a place of about 5 years, it have grow to be apparent to even the slowest-witted readers, writers and publishers, that the arrival of the Kindle (and similar devices) supposed that publishing had clearly long past through the most large trade because the discovery of printing.

I'm now not going to try to provide you with any specific concept of the numbers of posted books these days, because the statistics on e-book output are simply unreliable. I will certainly component out that in January 2012 David Houle suggested a conference that: 'There had been greater books published this week than there have been in all of 1950.' He won't were vain right, even to the nearest 10, however he end up in the proper ball park.

In 1990, there were some 25,000 books posted in the US, and the best certain detail is that numbers given that then have extended pretty. The growth has been powered in particular through the reality that new printing era has made it viable for authors to put up their personal books at highly reduced price.

According to Bowker, it in reality is the organization that handles ISBN numbers and unique bibliographical records, about 344,000 revealed e-book were posted in 2011, and forty three in keeping with cent of those had been self-published. In addition, at least 87,000 ebooks have been self-posted. These numbers are in all likelihood lower than the actual figures.

Formerly, the gates to e-book had been locked tight. You wanted a triple password, an endorsement from a more than one bestseller and a observe from your Mum in advance than genuinely every body could in all likelihood even concentrate on your plea for admission. But now – Amazon has opened a present day set of gates spherical the another time. These gates are stored sincerely open. And there may be a large sign over the pinnacle which says, 'Come on in, the water's lovable. We don't care in case you're not plenty cop at spelling, and there are in reality readers available who don't understand a semi-colon from a cold inside the head. All you want, to locate readers, is a chunk of a story – try it out, at our price, and see if every body likes it.'

Incidentally, with regards to bestsellers in ebooks, the most a fulfillment publishers, in 2013, had been unsurprisingly drawn from the Big Five. Using appearances at the Digital Book World ebook bestseller listing as our criterion, Hachette, Penguin, and Random House did quality. But, if we don't forget self-published authors as forming one indie publishing enterprise, the indie authors beat anybody else. Beat HarperCollins, Simon & Schuster, Macmillan, et al.

Chapter 6: The Espresso-Keep Printing System

And what, you will be questioning, of that different digital improvement which have become forecast with the beneficial useful resource of Jason Epstein across the flip of the century?

Epstein, you may recall, anticipated that earlier than prolonged there would be machines on each High Street (probably in espresso shops, sooner or later the name Espresso Book Machine) which could print you a duplicate of definitely any e-book interior a couple of minutes. Well, we're almost there.

In September 2012 it emerge as introduced that the Espresso Book Machine developers would be co-on foot with Eastman Kodak to contain those machines in Kodak Picture Kiosks in as a bargain as one zero five,000 places global.

And in case you haven't truly visible this form of machine however, neither have I. So it's no accurate pretending that this innovation has had the huge effect of the Kindle. Neither do I expect it ever will. It may moreover never show to be a probable commercial enterprise version. But the idea isn't lifeless but, and there are despite the fact that quite some human beings round who just like the concept.

Suppose you've in truth have a look at a cracking notable novel and you trust you studied your Aunty Jane would like a published duplicate for her birthday. Or, extra precisely, on the equal time as you meet her later on these days. It is probably tremendous, wouldn't it, if you can get one found out for your lunch hour?

Success stories of the digital age

When you be a part of the self-publishing community (the indie-publishers), you will be becoming a member of a few eminent company. In 2010, the advertising and marketing guru Seth Godin, writer of 12 print bestsellers which have been translated into 33 languages, announced that during future he is going to now not artwork through traditional publishers. He argues that, in an e-book international, there are possible methods of reducing publishers out of the loop out (a tool called disintermediation). Now he can obtain human beings virtually as correctly, if no longer greater so, without traditional publishers, and grow to be making extra cash.

Prior to coming to this quit, Seth were speakme to many set up print publishers and he have become unimpressed via way of way of what he placed. 'Most of them looked at me like I actually have turn out to be nuts for being an optimist. One CEO labored as tough as she need to to restrain herself, however failed and almost threw me out of her place of work thru the prevent. I'd be lying if I stated I wasn't heartbroken at the priority I observed.'

But there's no want for writers to be afraid. Quite the opposite. As I shall now show.

Before I circulate at once to provide an explanation for some achievement stories, permit me say that a fulfillment writers have constantly been the exception. By a big margin. And that is proper however you care to define the word 'a success'.

Success for some people in fact approach getting an article published in a magazine. Or triumphing the nearby writers' group month-to-month competition for a 10-line poem. For others, it manner promoting extra copies than Stephen King and

Danielle Steel mixed. Either manner, achievement is uncommon. And it want to no longer be taken into consideration inevitable. It isn't always a case of without a doubt do this, found through that, and plug it on Twitter and Facebook, and you're certain to hit the huge time. Never modified into, never can be.

Nevertheless, it's miles an established reality that some proficient writers have not simplest controlled to apply their talents within the digital age, however have moreover had the good fortune to be inside the right place at the proper time with the right e book.

The runaway successes of the digital age had been broadly publicised, and I am not going to do a high-quality deal greater proper right right here than point out a number of their names, absolutely in case you are a newbie to this game and function not come upon them earlier than.

You might like to have a look at the ones writers' net web sites and one-of-a-type blog posts et cetera about them.

To start with, it's well worth noting that Amazon itself often publicises the self-publishing successes, a great way to inspire others to apply their Kindle Direct Publishing centers. In early 2012, for instance, Amazon posted a listing of the top ten bestsellers on its internet site in 2011, combining the income of every print and e-book versions. Of those ten books, were novels that have been to be had in e-book shape handiest. And – vital issue – every those books had been self-posted. I'd in no way heard of both of them till I observed the Amazon listing. One became The Mill River Recluse, at quantity four, and the other became The Abbey, at enormous range 9.

The Mill River Recluse is through Darcie Chan. And whilst you look this woman up you locate that hers is an surely traditional story of the digital age. It took her three years to complete the book, and then she tested it out on her family and pals, polished it up, and despatched it out to standard publishers. Got actually nowhere. Scores of rejections. Sent it out to dozens of retailers, with the equal result. Then one top-beauty agent took her on (Laurie Liss at Sterling Lord). Laurie sent the e-book to all her top notch contacts, over a similarly -twelve months period. But though no sale.

By that point Darcie had grow to be aware about this new-fangled digital self-publishing commercial enterprise agency. So she gave it a attempt. Edited the ebook herself, did her non-public formatting, designed her very private cowl, and treated her very very own exposure.

The e-book was published in May 2011. In June, she end up pleased whilst a hundred copies had been sold. After that, aided thru some tough artwork on advertising, and a bit little little bit of marketing and advertising, topics commenced out to snowball, until inside the latter part of the year the ebook grow to be promoting severa thousand copies an afternoon.

This e-book changed into, it's well worth repeating, the fourth largest-promoting e-book at the whole of Amazon in 2011, and no longer the use of a paper model in any respect.

Other well-known self-publishers encompass Amanda Hocking, John Locke (the eighth writer, and the first self-published one, to promote over 1 million ebooks on Amazon), and Hugh Howey.

What distinguishes the ones books and their authors from 10000 others? Ah, if pleasant we knew. All we are in a position to mention, with any self belief, is that on occasion a ebook will discover its readers and in reality take off. But through and huge it acquired't.

Two-way website site visitors in the virtual age

An interesting phenomenon inside the virtual age is the two-manner internet site website online visitors amongst conventional publishing and indie publishing.

At a high-quality factor, some indie publishers who do truely the whole lot themselves have come to the perception that they'll in no way have any unfastened time, in no way stay a ordinary existence, till they locate someone to assist out with the everyday stuff.

Amanda Hocking, as an instance, have end up eventually furnished $2 million with the aid of way of St Martin's Press, to enter proper right into a conventional publishing affiliation with them. And why did she sign?

'I need to be a creator,' said Amanda. 'I do now not want to spend forty hours each week coping with emails, formatting covers, finding editors, and so forth.' In exclusive phrases, she dreams a person to do the guide labour for her.

Conversely, some well-known writers have in the long run well-known the factor made via Jason Epstein in Book Business, especially that they don't actually need a creator in any respect. If they have already got enjoy of the publishing approach, they may rent inside the assist as crucial. Barry Eisler, a mystery creator whose music record consists of a Gumshoe Award for Best Thriller of the Year, truely grew to turn out to be down a ultra-modern contract with St Martin's Press, properly well worth $500,000, and decided to govern his non-public destiny thereafter, as an indie.

Further down the famous and a success list, bear in mind the revel in of Elisabeth Naughton

Elisabeth is a surely interesting case-look at, due to the reality she started out her career in traditional publishing, operating via famous mass-marketplace organizations including Dorchester and Sourcebooks. Elisabeth end up in no manner a big dealer. She have end up what's called a mid-list author; or maybe decrease at the chain. Her contracts have been, as she locations it, crappy, but top day – she have grow to be a published author, OK? Respect! Prestige! Money! She had all the accolades of being a published author – her books have been on ebook location shelves and in airports, she modified into getting rave opinions, she end up a pinnacle company in romance for Sourcebooks, and he or she or he or he even hit the united states Today bestsellers listing.

But surely Elisabeth positioned that she become spending more money on selling her books than she became incomes in royalties. She used to visit romance readers' conferences and mix with the fans, spending money on air fares and inns. And she spent coins on promotional materials. So, after cautious perception, she backed a long way from traditional publishing. She were given her rights once more from Dorchester and feature grow to be an indie writer.

Tucked away on her difficult power Elisabeth had an unpublished book known as Wait for Me. This novel had been rejected by using the use of numerous literary sellers due to the fact, as they placed it, it straddled genres. But Elisabeth believed in it, and posted it herself in e-book shape. Wait for Me then proceeded to hit every critical e-book bestseller list, and it maintains to sell thoroughly.

In 2011, Elisabeth's tax pass lower back showed horrible earnings: in extraordinary terms, her costs as a creator amounted to extra than she earned. In 2012, as a self-writer, she said six figures on the high best facet; in 2013 she modified into drawing close the seven-determine mark. But recall – she wrote for ten years without developing a penny while costs had been considered.

In the United Kingdom, every different author, Janet MacLeod Trotter, has completed a whole lot the equal thing. In 2012, Janet's novel The Tea Planter's Daughter grow to be one of the pinnacle ten bestselling Kindle ebooks on Amazon.Co.Uk. And it's especially thrilling because of the reality this ebook has facts.

The clue to its history changed into supplied by using way of way of a assertion, at the Amazon web page for the ebook, that it modified into lengthy-listed for the Romantic Novelists' Association Romantic Novel of the Year Award in 2008. So it obviously wasn't a new e-book in 2012.

I preferred to recognize greater, and my first research prevent have become the catalogue of my neighborhood library. A search right here exhibits that this book changed into first posted by means of Headline in 2007, at the identical time as it had the call The Tea Planter's Lass; a paperback came from Headline a 3 hundred and sixty five days later. (Just in case you're new to this agency, let me say that Headline is a extremely good UK creator of company fiction, and plenty of authors would supply more than one tooth to be placed on their list.) In addition to the hardback and paperback versions, there also are CD and cassette versions of a speakme-e-book version, and a massive-print edition from Magna.

If you pass without delay to Janet MacLeod Trotter's private net internet web web page, evidently she is the author of 16 books that have been published thru Headline, starting in 1993; maximum of these fall into the family saga or ladies's fiction elegance. She also writes crime fiction under the call J.M. MacLeod.

Furthermore – and that is in which it begins offevolved to get actually interesting – Janet's internet site tells us that she now runs a 'micro publishing industrial corporation, specialising in paperbacks and ebooks.' Its name is MacLeod Trotter Books (MTB).

Back to Amazon another time, and we find out that MTB has 34 books on its list, alongside aspect the ones formerly published through Headline. And Headline, for its component, not lists Janet's name on its listing of authors.

So. The 2012 list of Amazon indie-author successes includes an author who has now seen the virtual mild, dropped all connection with antique-time publishing, and reissued a 'dead' e book 5 years later. By giving it a contemporary name and a ultra-contemporary cover (the usage of a circle of relatives photo), Janet has grew to become the radical proper right right into a pinnacle-ten e-book bestseller. In addition, she's self-publishing new versions of all her vintage output, in each digital and paperback versions, through her non-public imprint.

The destiny of traditional publishing

Today, each weblog and every ebook-worldwide communicate talk board is entire of hypothesis approximately the e-book-publishing international. Will the Big Five publishers (as they're now) bypass the way of the famous names in photos, and crumble into insolvency? And in that case, on the equal time as?

I am no longer going to feature to this hypothesis. If you're looking for evidence, to argue for survival and persevered prosperity at the best hand, or an early loss of life at the opportunity, it's miles tough to discover some thing honestly convincing. The Big Five placed out earnings reports which endorse persevered success. But then they may do this, wouldn't they? Immediately previous to disintegrate, and the call for for government bailouts, all of the huge banks have been very constructive of their public statements. And likewise you can discover analysts who see now not a few factor however decline in the Big Five figures –

such of them as they recollect. We shall see.

What I will say is that fiction, in particular, lends itself fairly to the e-book medium. And in case you are a novelist you may be unwise, in my view, to trouble with something apart from self-manual. On the alternative hand, if you are an educational historian and choice to put up a determined amount embodying the results of your ten years of research into the motives of the number one international struggle, then your amazing plan is simply to woo one of the extended-installation college presses, and to are attempting to find manual in posted shape (probably with maps and pictures, which ebooks absolutely can't deal with).

The simplest distinct aspect I will add is that writers are typically noticing that publishers are behaving as although they want to preserve cash. Faced with the opportunity of financial catastrophe, publishers are providing a terrific deal reduced advances closer to royalties. Furthermore, the blogger and novelist M.J. Rose evaluations from New York that publishers in the interim are trying to writers to provide their personal advertising charge variety! This is being dressed up as an funding of their personal competencies. And are the publishers presenting a larger royalty as compensation for this funding? Are they heck. Instead they're complaining that authors constantly were given too much of the coins except. This proposed monetary 'funding', please have a examine, is on pinnacle of the investment of time and energy which writers are already predicted to install with the aid of giving interviews and lectures, attending signing intervals, and so forth.

Chapter 7: What's A Horrible Writer To Do?

If you've examine as a protracted way as this, you're presumably a author of some type, and also you're probably inquisitive about full-duration fiction. You've been delivered as an lousy lot as enjoy that you truly acquired't be able to keep your head up in polite society besides you're published in determined out-ebook shape, ideally hardback, and visibly on sale in every book keep that your own family and pals are ever likely to enter.

Well, honest sufficient. It's a factor of view. It emerge as mine as quickly as. And if that's the way you need to move, purchase your self a duplicate of the Writers' and Artists' Yearbook (UK) or Writer's Market (US) and plunge in.

But there may be an opportunity, and the alternative is to turn out to be a self-author, or indie author. Start with Kindle, read up all of the recommendation that Amazon offers you (and there's quite a few it), and go with the flow your very private manner.

If you're smart sufficient to have written a singular, or maybe if you've truly idly placed this present e-book on a person's pill, you're actually clever sufficient to determine out the way to layout an ebook. You've got the hold of e mail and Word, haven't you? You know approximately RSS feeds, Paypal, stuff like that? OK, so that you can layout an e-book, in case you exercise your mind to it.

You can layout your very personal cowl too. Amazon gives you a fairly in reality way to do it. Or you can make your very non-public. Just download some free image-editing software program (GIMP will do well), or pay for Photoshop Elements, which is what I use. Yes, it does take time to discover ways to use this sort of software program, and also you want to steerage, but the extra you do the less hard it turns into. Nothing new approximately that. Same with the principle a part of the employer enterprise, that's writing a completely unique.

Then… whilst you've completed all that, at the same time as your indie book is out in advance than the admiring public, you sit down down decrease lower back and wait.

If no longer something an lousy lot takes region, you write a few extra and do it yet again. In reality you want to jot down some greater anyway, whilst you're ready. But if, thru the grace of a few aspect gods can be, you find out one million or readers, and appeal to a touch little bit of hobby, then perhaps an agent, or perhaps a creator, will approach you. And that's masses the brilliant manner round.

three.Nine Contracts are nasty... (insert impolite noun of desire)

It is a truth that, for properly over 100 years, e-book publishers have been blessed by means of using the life of a massive type of mugs, suckers, and various fuzzy thinkers, who have been inclined to work for a 12 months or , to provide a whole-duration manuscript on spec, without a penny piece to show for it. These should-be authors then dispatch their manuscript to a author, or an agent, who in a extraordinary quantity of instances proceeds to lose it; however even though the recipient keeps music of it, it's far quality to ship the aspect back, after a modest remove of six months or so, with a scrappy piece of paper saying 'Sorry – now not quite what we are searching out.'

So shabby and disgraceful is the enterprise's remedy of its authors that it is a small miracle, if fact be told, that publishers (and retailers) aren't every day visited with the aid of a small gang of infuriated slush-pile rejects, brandishing iron bars and sawn-off shotguns, annoying to appearance 'that son of a whinge who wrote this letter.'

However, permit us to assume, for a paragraph or two, that at a few diploma you are in truth provided a settlement with a 'expert' author.

Contracts require an entire e-book of their very personal, and there are a few such books to be had in case you poke round within the bibliographies and serps. I ought to have written one myself as soon as – in fact, with my creator's hat on, I wrote a few actual contracts in instances beyond – however I'm now not going to enter remarkable detail on contracts proper here because of the truth I experience I am obsolete.

I will, but, provide a few wide-brush feedback.

In america there is a attorney who specialises in contracts for the leisure media, and whose partner is an indie writer. The attorney's name is David Vandagriff, and he writes a weblog called The Passive Voice. Here's what he has to mention about ebook contracts: 'After having reviewed many, many agreements and proposed agreements among traditional publishers and authors, [I am] organized to mention those contracts, as a set, stand aside from the overall run of industrial commercial enterprise organisation agreements as experience of right and wrong-sudden monstrosities. They're genuinely designed to screw authors and to offer publishers manage over their work that is a prolonged manner beyond what's appeared as reasonably-priced within the relaxation of

American company.' (The UK isn't always any distinct, with the aid of using the manner.)

You must additionally look at what expert authors which include Dean Wesley Smith and his partner Kristine Kathryn Rusch have to mention on this problem. Both of them run blogs (see Appendix at the give up of this e book).

You ought to in fact hold an eye fixed on an internet site referred to as Writer Beware. This is run with the resource of the Science Fiction and Fantasy Writers of America, and we all owe them a terrific debt. They have an entire lot to mention on contracts with traditional publishers, and little of it's miles complimentary.

Here are some small suggestions to the type of issues you may probably stumble upon. Just examples.

At a while, probably even a long term after signing a settlement, you may want to supply the settlement to an stop, and reclaim rights that you as quickly as granted. But, in the present united states of america of things, you received't be capable of try this till the writer is unwell to loss of life of you, in which case you will had been dumped years within the beyond.

Modern publishers, as I truly have over and over stated, are quite rattling clueless at strolling a agency effectively. But one component I will grant them: they will be remarkably right at writing contracts which lock you to their bosom for ever – in the event that they simply need to keep you.

The reversion clause, as it's referred to as, can be nicely-nigh unbreakable. You gained't be capable of get your rights once more.

Then there's a clause which prevents you from presenting some aspect to some different author which might compete with the ebook you've offered to them (provided it for ever, as you presently recognize). So, in case you're a huge fulfillment as a romance writer, you could not be able to write any greater romances for a few other writer due to the fact the agreement forbids it. It's usually known as a non-competition clause, or some thing comparable.

And then, subsequently, you would probably obtain be aware about an addendum to the settlement, despatched to you thru the put up, or through e mail. You is probably asked to sign it.

One hassle can be confident: this addendum acquired't make the settlement any extra beneficial to you. Beware of addenda.

And then, of course, due to the fact massive publishing is locating it increasingly more tough to make profits in the vintage way, or perhaps inside the new way, they have all started out to dabble in cunning plans. If it's tough to get clients to shop for their books, why now not scrounge coins out of the writers? After all, in the event that they're dumb sufficient to spend years writing a ebook and are decided to get into print beneath the decision of a well-known and as soon as genuine employer, offer them the chance to perform that! For a rate, of route.

In 2012, Penguin supplied a agency called Author Solutions. This business agency have become widely recognized for supplying self-publishing services to writers – offerings for which they charged huge sums of coins. Want a 'internet-optimised press launch' for your e-book?

Certainly, sir or madam: which will be $1,199 please.

Prior to the Penguin purchase, the only hundred and fifty,000 clients of Author Solutions had been charged an average of $5,000 and on not unusual offered a hundred and fifty books.

In the equal 3 hundred and sixty 5 days, Simon & Schuster set up a subsidiary known as Archway Publishing, which they undergo in thoughts to run at the component of… certain, you guessed it, our vintage acquainted buddies Author Solutions. With costs beginning at $1600, Archway might do for authors that which they may perfectly well do for themselves for not some thing, specifically put up an ebook version.

Book-change commentators had been unimpressed. One such, Nate Hoffelder, wrote as follows:

'Author Solutions might be presently owned via Penguin, a detail which does now not talk nicely for Penguin's commercial organization ethics, however there can be no sign that they've cleaned up their act. All we're seeing nowadays is that Author Solutions is honestly imparting the same scammy offers as they constantly have, first-class this time they get to perform that below the previously right call of Simon & Schuster.'

Frankly, I develop weary of listing even a sample of the pitfalls of mixing with conventional publishers. So allow me end with the aid of using the use of telling you that I as soon as wrote a ebook referred to as The Truth about Writing. The first paragraph of that e-book ran as follows:

'Writing is an activity that could critically harm your fitness. It can consume huge portions of time and power, and it can bring about frustration, rage, and bitterness.' The ordinary motive of The Truth about Writing became, I said, 'to protect and keep the sanity of all of us who is unfortunate enough to be with the ambition to write down.'

What become true of my earlier ebook is proper of this one – the satisfactory that you're reading right now.

Above all, mother and father, try to have a laugh while you're writing. If it isn't amusing, write a few element else. Or do something else, together with taking long walks inside the u . S ..

And on the equal time as really each person like a touch achievement every now and then, fulfillment can be modest and however profitable. Read my essay On the Survival of Rats inside the Slush Pile, and discover ways to artwork to professional requirements at the same time as final an newbie.

Chapter 8: Traditional Vs. Indie Publishing

Let me start through explaining the distinction, basically, among conventional publishing and indie or self-publishing. It in fact boils down to standard publishing being centered on extra traditional, hooked up tropes and mind for books. Whereas, indie or self-publishing is greater of an anything is going option.

What I mean through that is, traditional publishers have great genres and tropes that they promote, due to the truth they may be centered on income. They are a large employer with loads of personnel and often stockholders to satisfy.

When at a series bookstall, the ones easy cover images everywhere are more regularly than no longer, theirs. If you task to a massive writer's internet web site, you could locate lists of genres they acquire in addition to facts approximately the gatekeepers you'll need to impress to discover your e-book in that chain ebook location.

As for indie, which I use in place of the phrase self-published, for indie moreover consists of small presses who have confined team of workers, the concept is certainly everyone can positioned up a few issue, and the ebook trying to find marketplace need to decide if it is a success.

Often you'll see indie books which may be circulate-style or out of the publishing norm like novellas and dinosaur porn (you genuinely don't want to recognize, however I'll offer you with a hyperlink except. You're welcome). Sometimes you'll find out novels with the useful resource of authors uninterested within the obstacles of traditional publishing or likely books via authors who's rights reverted again to them.

I began my career off as a traditionally posted author. I apprehend how difficult the adventure may be. I want your course to be less complex than mine become, that is why I decided to jot down down this guide. For I had no clue what I even have come to be getting myself into once I typed THE END.

Traditional Publishing

Traditional publishers are what most humans don't forget once they don't forget an writer. They think popularity and fortune. Of booksignings and jet-putting round the sector.

If handiest.

I blame TV for this. Shows like Castle are a super example. Richard Castle changed into a creator who lived in a NY metropolis loft and went to fancy activities.

Can't say I've ever been invited to a fancy birthday party. Maybe I should strive a unique deodorant…

That being said, your odds of wealth and repute are a bit better with a traditional publisher as they've the infrastructure as well as advertising price range to help you get there. They additionally have the only key factor an indie creator commonly lacks, distribution. It's hard to come to be a success if you aren't moving into the the front of readers.

When I say conventional publisher, I'm, in maximum times, regarding a Big five creator like Penguin Random House (Big five publishers manner the top five media conglomerates publishing books within the US.) or a mid-sized one like Kensington Books. A smaller press can be a conventional press, inside the event that they pay an increase and function in-house advertising and advertising and marketing.

The way to get your e-book within the the the front of acquisition editors (AKA the those who buy your manuscript and flip it right into a e-book) is usually with the aid of getting yourself an agent, who then tactics the editor. Without an agent, no matter the truth that the author accepts unsolicited and unagented manuscripts, your query/manuscript may come to be in the slush pile.

And bear in mind me in this, editors not regularly advantage the lowest of the pile.

Your manuscript might languish for 6 months to from time to time years. Given the amount of hard paintings an acquisitions editor already has, how some of a glance does a slush manuscript get? A net page? Or lots an awful lot less?

That manner, a) your first few pages ought to be ideal and b) find an agent who can paintings their relationships with editors to get you extra than a thirty-second study.

Before we try this, allow us to have a look at why you'll traditionally positioned up, aside from the Castle-like repute.

Pros of Publishing Traditionally

We'll begin with the large one—THE ADVANCE.

An enhance is coins paid via manner of the writer for you agreeing to have them buy your book. It's form of like a mortgage in a few approaches, an quantity they may be risking if income are bad and you don't earn out (I'll offer an purpose of what incomes out manner in a bit).

In some cases, even though uncommon, writers have had to pay decrease lower back their enhance, but commonly in instances in which the e-book is unacceptable following the editorial letter (again, I'll provide an purpose at the back of that later too).

When I commenced, the normal fashion pick out improve became somewhere amongst $five,000 and $15,000 (usually the lower of which). Seeing as inflation has increased…

Yep, you obtain it. Chances are you'll get across the identical these days.

If you get an boom the least bit.

Plenty of publishers are moving to a royalty charge fine (this is better) and print-on-call for (POD). But those aren't generally the Big 5. It is a modern-day style in the corporation so who's aware about what is going to display up inside the following few years.

Another pro of traditional publishing is the infrastructure. They have in-residence editors--acquisitions and copy, PR humans, sales departments, formatters, printers, and masses of employees running on making your manuscript right proper into a ebook.

And, as I mentioned earlier than, traditional publishers have various channels of distribution. If your dream is to look your e-book in a book place like Barnes & Noble, then you definitely pretty a bargain have handiest one opportunity, it truly is to put up traditionally.

There are techniques to get your indie ebook at B&N. I circulate over those inside the indie publishing manual additionally available. Furthermore, conventional publishers will regularly pay to have their probably bestsellers inside the first-class sections of the e-book region.

As with distribution, your possibilities of getting on a bestseller list are extra being historically published. I'm no longer regarding Amazon bestseller lists, but lists like The New York Times and Publishers Weekly. Those lists are developed primarily based on earnings at certain bookstores at some stage in america of a. So despite the fact that an indie creator supplied a few hundred thousand copies on Amazon, they possibly wouldn't hit the ones lists.

One more benefit of publishing historically is the backing of in-house promoting. But recognize this, the amount of promotional greenbacks are right now associated with how properly your ebook is idea to sell. Therefore, a debut writer like yourself receives a whole lot lots much less in terms of advertising and marketing and advertising bang than an writer with an extended and colourful profits statistics.

That doesn't imply your in-house PR person acquired't be fantastic. It just way, possibilities are, they won't have as lots time or strength in your e-book.

Not that during-residence advertising technique loads these days, as the writer is accountable for ninety% in their ebook vending except—the entirety from the discharge, to social media, to advertising, to putting in area booksignings and shopping for SWAG for giveaways.

Your in-residence PR will likely deliver out evaluation replica requests and probably setup some interviews. Often they will proportion your occasions on the writer's social media. Don't count on a good deal as a debut. It's up to you to promote your self and your books.

A traditional author will frequently provide packing containers of ARC (moreover known as galley copies) that permits you to deliver to reviewers to your non-public. They additionally provide completed copies too, based totally totally mostly on your agreement. I've gotten bins of 100 to as little as copies. It all relies upon.

Finally, the most essential seasoned for traditional publishing—No in advance costs.

A right traditional creator will NEVER ask you to offer them money. If they do, you're probably dealing with a vanity press. I endorse you avoid the ones in any respect rate. Even if you decide at the indie direction, you could rent humans to do the equal artwork the conceitedness creator gives for a brilliant deal a good buy much less.

Chapter 9: Cons Of Publishing Traditionally

Now for the much less exquisite factors of conventional publishing. Again, permit's talk coins first. Royalty expenses are often less than outstanding in evaluation to indie publishing who generally tend to pinnacle out spherical 70%.

Typical royalty expenses of mainstream, traditional publishers:

Hardcover

 10% - 15% normal with reproduction

Trade Paper

 7% regular with duplicate

E-e-book

25% in step with replica

What that ruin proper all of the manner down to in money to your pocket:

Hardcover

$25 retail = $2.50-$3.00 for the writer constant with e-book provided

Trade Paper

$15 retail = about $1.00 for the author consistent with e-book presented

E-ebook

$five retail = $1.25 for the author steady with e-book furnished

The truth it takes 2 – three years to appearance your ebook in print, from at the same time as you sign the settlement, is a huge con.

It took me 4 years to get an agent, then 2 more to sell my first e-book, and a couple of greater after that to appearance it in print. That's 8 years, not which include ways prolonged it took to research sufficient craft to put in writing a first rate sized and plotted ebook.

For me, that become 6 years.

For a complete of 14 years earlier than my first ebook fell proper right into a reader's hand.

Mind you, your adventure is not mine. You may additionally write a outstanding ebook in six months, and get an agent and ebook deal in every different 3 hundred and sixty 5 days.

That nevertheless approach three ½ years until you notice any royalties.

Keeping a day interest or marrying for coins is making some of experience now, huh?

Another con is having to skip via the gatekeepers to get your manuscript look at via the writer. Those gatekeepers include sellers and acquisition editors.

With 200 million people trying to be the following J.K. Rowlings, gatekeepers assist defend the publishers from being inundated with poorly crafted manuscripts and crazy human beings.

Given that you've crafted a outstanding story and aren't in any respect insane, ramming up in the direction of gatekeepers can be very annoying. In truth, it's possibly the worst element of publishing.

When selecting the right course, you want to test important troubles. First of this is, when you signal a publishing agreement, you have got were given got, for all intents and capabilities, supplied your ebook. Meaning, you have were given were given little to no input until specially requested through the publisher in revision, duplicate modifying, manufacturing and advertising and marketing. It is now the publishers ebook, not yours, despite the fact that your name is on the quilt.

That technique, if you hate the quilt, you may whinge (in spite of the truth that you possibly shouldn't). Or say they want a positive passage eliminated or even a whole character. It's their ebook now. Not yours. Most of the time, it obtained't come to blows. Publishers commonly are attempting to find the writer's enter. Note, I said, USUALLY.

That moreover signifies, they very very own the content too (besides you specially saved high quality rights). You can't write books with the equal characters, and occasionally inside the same worlds without unique permission and primary rights of refusal (because of this what it appears like—the author has the risk at some thing e-book in a sequence with the ones characters/international earlier than you can publish it with a person else or to your personal). Sometimes they'll hold the proper to observe a few thing ebook you write next before each person else can.

And eventually, we come to profits. If you don't earn out (which means that, sell sufficient books to cover the development based totally on the royalty charges, i.E. $1 on every $15 change paperback) then your destiny in publishing, as a minimum in writer call, may be in jeopardy.

Authors who don't promote properly fade into obscurity, reborn in some different call. I realise authors who're on their fourth or 5th name.

Keep in mind, you've got got were given little within the way of in-house advertising aid. The great way to get more marketing and advertising and marketing bucks is to promote more books.

Traditional Publishing – The Steps

Both traditional publishing and indie have awesome steps to observe which will have the first-rate risk at fulfillment. The following are those associated with publishing on a extra traditional route.

Step 1 — The Manuscript

The everyday format used for while you want an agent or editor to view your manuscript is as follows:

•ONE document (Word .Doc or .Docx is commonly great)

•1 inch margins

•Courier New or Times New Roman Font – 12 element

•Paragraphs should be set to cling first line at .05

•Double spaced

•Italics are underlined Example: I love him ought to look like this in your manuscript, I love him.

•Scene breaks are indicated with #

•New chapters begin 1/three net net web page down (extra or less four inches)

•Chapters headings are targeted, the whole lot else is left justified.

•Never use capitals for emphasis like I DO in the course of this guide.

Before a manuscript is marketable, it desires to be within the pleasant shape viable. Sometimes, as a extremely-contemporary creator, that's hard to pick out in your personal. In that case, I propose using your creator-buddies that will help you. Join writer corporations. You can look at tons from distinctive writers further to make life-long connections. Who else will solution the mobile phone inside the useless of night time time when you have a query on in which to bury a frame…?

Hopefully not any of your non-author friends.

Critique groups also are a fantastic useful useful resource for information what's running in your manuscript and what won't be. It can be tough to get rid of your ego and distinct people's egos from critiquing. Feelings get harm. It's natural. This is your toddler. Your brain-infant.

I recognize really.

Now I want you to pay attention and HEED my story. I received over 1,000 rejections in advance than I posted my first book. A ebook that changed into the fifth one I'd wrote. Had I completed a higher process of taking note of evaluations, it might've lessened the sheer amount of rejection.

I'm no longer announcing, be aware of the whole thing everyone says for there can be clearly as an awful lot wrong with that, however be affordable in terms of your art work.

NO ONE writes an splendid 1st draft, despite the fact that they could anticipate so.

Half the warfare is in revision.

Then comes duplicate/line edits.

And analyzing your ebook for the millionth time, till you hate each comma.

Only then are you geared up for Step 2….

Step 2 — Getting an Agent

There are hundreds of literary sellers to be had. Some are awesome, have scores of earnings and make their authors a bunch of cash. Some are real, quality people with the best intentions of creating authors and themselves cash. Others are cheats and liars who take gain of an creator's desperation. And a pick out out few, at the same time as nicely-intentioned, are just horrific at their jobs.

The question will become, how do you discover an sincere and affective agent?

It's now not that tough to find out an agent with a awesome income record. It calls for studies and a willingness not to accept a smooth positive from all of us claiming to be an agent. Let's deal with the primary element—Researching entrepreneurs. Like any extraordinary research, it starts offevolved with google.

I'm kidding. Sort of.

What I really need you to do is visit QueryTracker. It's loose to sign up for up and is a quite honest beneficial beneficial aid.

Publishers Marketplace is likewise a super beneficial aid, which includes such things as agent desire-lists and earnings facts. Though it's usually a for-pay net web page. At this element in your profession it may not be definitely well worth the price. But take a look at it out for the unfastened stuff they provide.

You'll be searching out sellers that suit your style. If you're no longer positive what that might be, go with the flow for the larger classes. Ask your self, is that this particularly a romance? A delusion? A thriller? Too regularly new writers get tied up in what style their ebook is, because of the reality EVERY query ebook or submit you observe tells you that you need to recognise it all the manner right down to the sub-style.

This manual can be awesome. Yes, it is outstanding to recognize your fashion due to the reality then you may aim your question more efficaciously. But it isn't a want.

Definitions of maximum not unusual commercial fiction genres:

•Classic – fiction that has grow to be a part of an full-size literary canon, drastically taught in colleges

•Crime/detective – fiction about a criminal offense, how the criminal receives stuck, and the repercussions of the crime

•Fable – mythical, supernatural story demonstrating a useful truth

•Fairy tale – story approximately fairies or unique magical creatures

•Fan fiction – fiction written via keen on, and providing characters from, a particular TV collection, film, or e-book   *pretty difficult to sell to any publisher because the rights to the authentic art work ought to need to be certified.

•Fantasy – fiction with peculiar or otherworldly settings or characters; fiction which invites suspension of reality

•Fiction narrative – literary works whose content material material is produced via the imagination and isn't always generally primarily based mostly on truth

•Historical fiction – tale with fictional characters and activities in a historical setting

•Horror – fiction in which sports activities evoke a feel of dread and on occasion worry in every the characters and the reader

•Humor – Usually a fiction whole of fun, fancy, and satisfaction, intended to entertain and every now and then reason intended laughter; but may be contained in all genres

•Magical realism – tale in which magical or unreal factors play a herbal element in an in any other case sensible environment

•Mystery – that is fiction managing the answer of a criminal offense or the unraveling of secrets and techniques

•Picture ebook – photo storybook is a ebook with very little phrases and some of images, picture tales are generally for little kids

•Science fiction – story based totally totally on the impact of actual, imagined, or capability technological understanding, normally set within the future or on exclusive planets

•Short tale – fiction of such brevity that it supports no subplots

•Suspense/mystery – fiction about damage about to befall someone or company and the tries made to steer clean of the damage

•Western – set inside the American Old West frontier and usually set within the late eighteenth to overdue nineteenth century

If the above list didn't help, please recognise that a primary style like romance, technological expertise fiction, mystery or literary is simply superb whilst querying.

Still not positive? Ask folks that've have a have a look at it what they suppose. Or query the nearest entrepreneurs to the style you get hold of as actual in conjunction with your novel suits in. If they may be looking for delusion and also you experience that simply might be your fashion, strive it. Agents, for the maximum element, will will will permit you to understand while you're off-base.

Now that you comprehend your style, have a examine dealers who a) represent that style, b) are actively seeking out new customers, c) have a confirmed sales track record. These are your pinnacle tier dealers. The ones you need to question first.

Another way to discover the satisfactory match is to look at novels like yours, particularly the acknowledgements internet web page. Often writers will reference sellers and editors. For the extra well-known authors, like J.K. Rowlings, opportunities are her agent obtained't be accepting new clients due to the reality, she or he likely doesn't need the money for one trouble. For lesser regarded sellers, this is a super way to discover them and get yourself up to speed with the names of publishing insiders.

Chapter 10: The Hook (Aka The Tagline)

We'll begin with an clean exercise to help you develop your hook. Read the movie hooks/tagline under. Can you bet what films they arrive from?

A drama critic learns on his wedding ceremony day that his cherished maiden aunts are homicidal maniacs, and that insanity runs in his family.

This is the tagline from the 1944 hit comedy and actually one among my all-time preferred films, Arsenic and Old Lace. If you didn't get that one, I apprehend, it's an vintage film. Let's have a take a look at this next one:

The getting older patriarch of an organized crime dynasty transfers manage of his clandestine empire to his reluctant son.

This is the tagline from any other conventional, The Godfather. Did the prepared crime provide it away? Would

171

you need to look it primarily based absolutely absolutely at the 18-word descriptor? One greater instance of a a fulfillment film and hook:

A teenage woman risks the entirety at the equal time as she falls in love with a vampire.

Yep, you guessed it. This hook is from the bestselling ebook and film, Twilight. Honestly as I examine it, it looks like one of these common hook, I doubt it'd grasp an agent's hobby, although it positive did readers and moviegoers alike.

Now it is your flip. I want you to brainstorm at least five hook/taglines using the subsequent as hints.

You meet an agent in the elevator. And the agent asks what is your ebook approximately?

•Make your hook/tagline 30 phrases or lots much less

•Use specific description in place of character names

•Focus on primary plotline

•Make it catchy

Simple, right?

Here's my tagline for CURSES!

When Cinderella is murdered, her not-so-unpleasant stepsister mistakenly hires an evilly-impotent villain to treatment the crime.

My tagline tells the agent/editor/reader what fashion the e-book is, who the primary characters are, and recommendations on the fundamental warfare/plot.

Amazing what 17 phrases can do.

I did damage my private rules with the aid of the use of the right name Cinderella. I allow you to understand this for two motives. The first is, that occasionally a right name, mainly if drastically diagnosed like Cinderella, is a better descriptor than an define. And secondly, understand that it's miles excellent to interrupt 'guidelines' of querying, much like those of writing, if it's far what's incredible.

Feel like you have have been given a hook? Run them with the aid of manner of your buddies and family. Even better run it thru strangers with out a chunk of bias. How did they react? Did they get a enjoy of your novel, and in that case, modified into their feel on issue?

At this point, you might be wondering why a hook/tagline is important to writing a question. I swear it's far. Trust me. I'm a author.

Hopefully in the next segment, it's going to start to make enjoy.

Writing the Query Letter

If you haven't test a question or don't recognize what an exquisite one seems like, I advocate you're taking a peek at Agent Janet Reid's Query Shark. It's an super useful resource.

That being stated, it'd additionally supply you right away right into a panic. So my idea is take a deep breath, examine a query or , after which strive your hand at writing your non-public. If you try and weed thru all of Janet's recommendation, your head will explode, and no man or woman needs that, especially in case you're in proximity to innocent, non-writers.

Here's the identical antique querying format for a commercial enterprise fiction challenge:

- Single spaced

- Less than 250 terms

- Times or Courier New font – 12 factor

- 1st Paragraph

  o The HOOK (This is your tagline)

- 2nd Paragraph

  o The story (Big photo, a good deal much less than 75 words)

- 1/three Paragraph

  o Bio (Writing relevant ONLY)

- *****Sign off with contact information*****

- Unless in any other case recommended on the agent's internet web page, encompass first 5 pages of MS at the prevent, not as an attachment.

•Never embody attachments even though photographs from your signature line.

Yep, you examine that proper. Less than 250 terms. If your hook is 30, and also you're fantastic allowed 75 more for large plot within the 2nd paragraph, you could see how essential each word will become.

I'll dive into all 3 sections a hint greater below, but for now, I desired to speak about the bio and writing applicable credit most effective. More frequently than not, new writers encompass a chunk about how they're new or that that is their first e-book. I don't endorse doing each. Let your writing communicate for you.

Why deliver a person a bias in advance than they examine the primary phrase of your manuscript?

The Query Letter

The first phase of the question, as I mentioned above, is all about the hook. Here's an instance from my very own question letter which received my agent over. It's for a e-book, which turn out to be later posted as Holy Socks & Dirtier Demons:

What do a reluctant hero, a narcissistic angel, a Zen-spouting Buddhist, and a demonic feminist have in not unusual, why the search for a abducted Baby Jesus in New York City, of direction. So starts offevolved offevolved offevolved my town delusion manuscript, The 2nd Coming, complete at 90 five,000 terms.

The first sentence is my hook. I don't recommend starting your query with a question like I did. Read Janet Reid's Query Shark and you'll see it's a brilliant domestic canine peeve of hers and masses of different dealers. My agent have come to be type of recent, so maybe it didn't problem her masses as it does those who have been in company for decades. I believe after a few years of reading slush, shops have seen the whole lot.

I furnished my style, the find out and the very last phrase count number right after the hook. Use your phrase processing software software phrase rely. When I started I spent hours identifying what number of terms consistent with discovered word rely (which is prepared 250 in step with internet page) most effective to find out, maximum sellers and editors can also need to care plenty much less. The manuscript you present to them gained't be the same one you promote. Word counts will exchange as revisions happen.

Brief apart about phrase depend. The agency has pointers on what every fashion's phrase rely range need to be. It doesn't damage to head over or beneath via some thousand. Sometimes the tale needs to be counseled, word bear in thoughts be dammed.

*If you've written a e-book over one hundred and fifty,000 phrases, as a debut creator, it's far going to be a difficult promote irrespective of your style.

•Literary - eighty,000 to one hundred ten,000

•Mystery/Thrillers - 70,000 to ninety,000

•Romance - 40,000 to one hundred,000

•Fantasy - ninety,000 to one hundred,000

•Paranormal/Urban - seventy five,000 to ninety five,000

•Horror - eighty,000 to one hundred,000

•Science-Fiction - 90,000 to a hundred twenty 5,000

•Historical - 100,000 to one hundred and twenty,000

•Young Adult (YA) - 50,000 to eighty,000

•Middle Grade (MG) - 30,000 to 50,000

Two crucial topics to phrase. I use the word whole. NEVER supply a question on something however a finished novel until you are writing a non-fiction e-book concept (it's an entire special kettle of fishes). And secondly, I name my e-book a manuscript. This is substantial as we often use the word ebook and manuscript interchangeably as writers. Your manuscript is NOT a e-book until it is posted.

And for the sake of all this is holy, don't are attempting to find recommendation from a novel as a fiction novel. A novel with the useful resource of definition is a bit of fiction. Most dealers hate the time period fiction novel and can be far an entire lot less willing to look at on after seeing it. It is so clean to show an agent off in advance than they ever have a look at a sentence of your manuscript. Be as professional as viable and also you're earlier of the game.

The Query Letter

The second phase of your query letter is an boom of the hook, into the plot and every now and then subplot, and deeper reasons for the characters. Again, below seventy five terms in standard. Hard to even reflect onconsideration on, proper? Think of it as an awful lot much less is greater, and further concrete is even higher.

The Messiah and his dad or mum angel arrive on the doorstep of Jace Miller, a disgruntled former soldier who has the same opinion to guard the Son of God from the forces of evil brewing beneath the City. He enlists a private investigating succubus after Jesus is abducted. Faced with demons, monsters, and a growing preference for the demon PI, Jace learns how mysterious the Almighty may be as he searches Heaven, Hell, and Newark for the Second Coming.

It is available in precisely at 75 phrases. I can also want to've used one hundred or so more. I'm certain you can too. If you want greater, than use extra. But hold in thoughts the 250 rule. A query letter ought to NEVER pass over 1 internet web page, single spaced.

The different crucial element to be aware is the voice. The voice ought to in form the tone of your e-book.

You don't need to preserve to the 3 paragraph fashion on your question. This segment may be more than one paragraph if that fits your fashion/voice.

A question must offer the agent with an understanding of your voice and fashion earlier than analyzing a word of your novel.

Most importantly, a query, like a synopsis, is constantly written in present demanding regardless of what stressful your manuscript is written in.

The Query Letter –

And the very last section is all about you as a author.

But you might be pronouncing, I haven't any writing credit score, what am I speculated to do?

First, try to get some. Writing short tales for journals and anthologies is a valid way to observe craft and get the ones e-book credit.